CW00816330

THE WEALTH OF ANGLO-SAXON ENGLAND

The Wealth of Anglo-Saxon England

Based on the Ford Lectures delivered in the
University of Oxford in Hilary Term 1993

PETER SAWYER

OXFORD
UNIVERSITY PRESS

OXFORD
UNIVERSITY PRESS

Great Clarendon Street, Oxford, OX2 6DP,
United Kingdom

Oxford University Press is a department of the University of Oxford.
It furthers the University's objective of excellence in research, scholarship,
and education by publishing worldwide. Oxford is a registered trade mark of
Oxford University Press in the UK and in certain other countries

British Library Cataloguing in Publication Data
Data available

ISBN 978-0-19-925393-7

Printed in Great Britain by
MPG Books Group, Bodmin and Kings's Lynn

PREFACE

The Ford Lectures on which this book is based were delivered in 1993. The delay has been partly due to previous commitments and the disruption caused by two removals, to Trondheim in 1996 and to Uppsala in 2006. In 2008 I began revising the first version in the light of very helpful comments by a reader for the Press, but this work was soon interrupted for two years by a serious illness. I have tried, with incomplete success, to take account of publications that have appeared since 1993.

In the first place I wish to thank the electors to the Ford Lectureship for inviting me. Many friends and colleagues have helped to keep me up to date by sending references and supplying books and papers, many in advance of publication. I am particularly grateful to Mark Blackburn and Stewart Lyon for criticizing early drafts of several chapters, and for the guidance they, together with Michael Metcalf, Martin Allen, and Rory Naismith, have given on the numismatic evidence. Stewart Lyon has kept me informed about the progress of his work on the Winchester and York mints, and has generously allowed me to use his results in advance of their publication. Thanks are also due to many others who have, at various stages, helped with advice and criticism: Marion Archibald, Martin Biddle, John Blair, Wolfgang Brockner, Nicholas Brooks, Donald Bullough, James Campbell, Simon Coupland, Michael Dolley, David Dumville, Christopher Dyer, Robin Eagleton, Mary Garrison, Malcolm Godden, James Graham-Campbell, Dennis Green, Philip Grierson, Sally Harvey, Gert Hatz, Joyce Hill, Kenneth Jonsson, Derek Keene, Susan Kelly, Jane Kershaw, Simon Keynes, Susan Kruse, Michael Lapidge,

John Latham, Kevin Leahy, John LePatourel, John Maddicott, Brita Malmer, John Moore, Janet Nelson, John Newman, Pamela Nightingale, Terence O'Connor, Elizabeth Pirie, Nigel Ramsey, Timothy Reuter, Dieter Rosenthal, Harold Schneider, Richard Sharpe, Ian Short, Colin Smith, Ian Stewart (Lord Stewartby), Katharina Ulmschneider, Alan Vince, Leslie Webster, Ian Wood, Patrick Wormald, and Ulrich Zwicker. I am also indebted to Kungl. Vetenskaps- och Vitterhets-Samhället i Göteborg for grants that enabled me to discuss this work with colleagues in England and to use the Sackler Library in Oxford.

My greatest debt is to my wife for her enthusiastic support from the start in 1989. She has patiently read, and criticized, several versions of the whole book. The result, however imperfect, is much the better for her advice.

CONTENTS

LIST OF FIGURES

For permission to reproduce illustrations, thanks are due to The Syndics of the Fitzwilliam Museum, Cambridge (figs. 1, 4, 5, 6, 9, 10, 12); Cambridge University Press (figs. 2, 3); Oxbow Books (fig. 7); British Numismatic Society (figs. 8, 11).

All coins are shown at double their original size.

LIST OF TABLES

LIST OF ABBREVIATIONS

For further details see References.

As   Laws of Athelstan; ed. F. Lieberann, *Gesetze*, 146–83; F. L. Attenborough, *Laws*, 122–69

ASC   *The Anglo-Saxon Chronicle*

ASE   *Anglo-Saxon England*

Atr   Laws of Æthelred; ed. F. Liebermann, *Gesetze*, 217–70; A. J. Robertson, *Laws*, 52–133

BAR   British Archaeological Reports

BNJ   *British Numismatic Journal*

Cn   Laws of Cnut; ed. F. Liebermann, *Gesetze*, 273–371; A. J. Robertson, *Laws*, 140–219

CTCE   C. Blunt, B. H. I. H. Stewart, and C. S. S. Lyon, *Coinage in Tenth-Century England*

CUHB   D. M. Palliser (ed.), *The Cambridge Urban History of Britain*

DB   Domesday Book, 2 vols GDB and LDB

Edg   Laws of Edgar; F. Liebermann, *Gesetze*, 192–215; A. J. Robertson, *Laws*, 16–39.

Edw   Laws of Edward the Elder; ed. F. Liebermann, *Gesetze*, 138–45: F. L. Attenborough, *Laws*, 114–21.

EHD   D. Whitelock (ed.), *English Historical Documents* 1, 2nd edn

EHR   *English Historical Review*

EMC	Early Medieval Coin Finds from the British Isles, 410–1180: <www.medievalcoins.org>
Encyclopaedia	The Blackwell Encyclopaedia of Anglo-Saxon England, ed. M. Lapidge et al.
GDB	Great Domesday Book
HE	Bede, Historia Ecclesiastica Gentis Anglorum
LDB	Little Domesday Book
MEC	P. Grierson and M. Blackburn, Medieval European Coinage
Med. Arch.	Medieval Archaeology
MGH	Monumenta Germaniae Historica
	Epist. Epistolae
	SRG Scriptores rerum germanicarum in usum scholarum
	SRM Scriptores rerum merovingicarum
	SS Scriptores
NC	Numismatic Chronicle
NCMH	The New Cambridge Medieval History
S	P. H. Sawyer, Anglo-Saxon Charters: An Annotated List and Bibliography
TRE	Tempore Regis Edwardi
TRHS	Transactions of the Royal Historical Society
VCH	Victoria Histories of the Counties of England

1

Introduction

One of the main purposes of this book is to explain how, on the eve of the Norman Conquest, England had become an exceptionally wealthy, highly urbanized kingdom, with a large, well-controlled coinage of high quality. As many texts and material remains tend to focus attention on things of great value, it is worth bearing in mind the wider definition of wealth offered by J. S. Mill in 1848 as 'all useful or agreeable things which possess exchangeable value...except those that can be obtained without labour or sacrifice'.[1] Most things, including land, had exchangeable value. Aldfrith, king of Northumbria (686–705), gave eight hides of land to Jarrow in exchange for a fine cosmography that Benedict Biscop had bought in Rome.[2] Three hundred years later Ælfric Bata composed a colloquy (quoted in Chapter 5) representing a customer for a manuscript offering to pay 'either in gold, or in silver, or in horses or mares or cows or sheep or pigs or goats or clothing or in wine or honey or grain or vegetable produce'—the scribe asked for cash (*denarios*).

In Anglo-Saxon England, as in other parts of Early Medieval Europe, the moveable wealth coveted by rulers, powerful men and

---

[1] *Oxford English Dictionary*, s.v. 'wealth'.
[2] Bede, *Historia Abbatum*, cap. 15.

women, and major churches was treasure. In an illuminating discussion of the role of treasure in Anglo-Saxon society, James Campbell points out that if the landed estates of a ruler could only produce 'food, rents and labour services, then the essentials for power had to be got elsewhere, that is, by taking them from those who already had them. In short he had to survive by war, so that retinues attracted by treasure-giving could be used to fight the battles which secured new treasure, thus establishing a kind of beneficent circle which was bound in the end to break.'[3] It is, however, one of the main arguments of this study that all the gold and almost all the silver in Anglo-Saxon England was imported. Some came as gifts, and in the late ninth and early tenth centuries Viking settlers brought a great deal that they had acquired in Francia, but most was the result of trade, as payment for exported produce.

Apart from coins, very little Anglo-Saxon treasure has survived, but the many descriptions, mainly of church treasures, gathered by Charles Dodwell show clearly that they were not only abundant, but that many must have been made by highly skilled craftsmen and women.[4] They also show that from the seventh century to the eleventh many donors to churches were remarkably rich in gold, silver, jewellery, fine textiles, and other valuable things. The treasure accumulated in Anglo-Saxon England had a profound influence on its history by attracting Scandinavian raiders for 300 years and Normans in 1066. It is also good evidence that exports from England were already substantial and profitable in the early eighth century, as they were 300 years later. That surprising conclusion is consistent with the numismatic evidence discussed in Chapter 3 where reasons are given for thinking that there were more coins circulating in eastern England in the first

[3] Campbell, 'The sale of land', 242.
[4] Dodwell, *Anglo-Saxon Art*. Much of the surviving treasure is illustrated in Webster and Backhouse, *The Making of England*.

years of the eighth century than at any other time before the Norman Conquest.

The value of numismatic evidence for early English history has been greatly enhanced by recent developments. Before the 1970s almost all the coins available for study in museums and private collections came from hoards, high-status graves, or excavations in towns, monasteries, and other important sites, but now a huge and increasing number of coins that were apparently lost accidentally are being found by metal detector users. By 2000 at least 6500 single coins struck between 600 and 1180 had been found and registered. In 2009 Michael Metcalf estimated that the number of silver coins known as sceattas made in the Lower Rhineland, Frisia, and England between c.670 and c.750 found in England 'at present being offered for sale on ebay, alas without provenance, amounts to at least two or three hundred a year'.[5] The dramatic rate of new discoveries is well illustrated by Derek Chick's study of the coins struck in southern England in Offa's reign (757–796). Over half the 723 coins, almost all single finds that he was able to catalogue in 2006 were found after 1959. By 2010 another 63 had been recorded.[6]

Single coin finds show where they were used and the discovery of several, in some cases struck over a long period, in a small area together with buckles, strap ends, ornaments, pins, and other artefacts probably indicate where markets were held. They are also a rough guide to changes in the size and composition of the coinage. For example, they suggest that there was a dramatic reduction in the number of coins in circulation for several decades after c.740 and that after that date imported coins no longer circulated freely in England. English coins were then the only legal tender until the end of the ninth century when coins imported by or made for Scandinavian

---

[5] Metcalf, 'Betwixt sceattas', 6.

[6] Chick, *Coinage of Offa*, 185–6; Naismith, 'Coinage of Offa revisited'. See also the Appendix.

invaders began to circulate in areas they controlled. In the tenth century the descendants of Scandinavian settlers were gradually forced to submit to the surviving Anglo-Saxon dynasty, and in 959 Alfred's great grandson, Edgar, was acknowledged as the sole ruler of Anglo-Saxon England.

At the end of his reign, probably in 973, the unity of the kingdom was clearly demonstrated by a fundamental reform of the coinage.[7] With rare exceptions there was only one denomination, the silver penny, which was struck in at least 50 mints. The fineness and weight of these coins were restored to the standards set a hundred years earlier by Alfred, and all had the same design, a stylized royal portrait with the king's name on the obverse, and a small cross surrounded by the names of the moneyer and mint on the reverse (see Figure 1a). This proved to be the start of a remarkably sophisticated system of monetary control that, despite Danish and Norman conquests, lasted until the early twelfth century.[8] The design of this reformed coinage was continued under Edgar's immediate successors, Edward the Martyr and Æthelred II, until c.979 when it was replaced by a new type with a hand on the reverse. Ten years later this was replaced by a new type, known as *Crux* because the reverse has these letters in the angles of a cross (Figure 1b). Thereafter the type was changed initially at intervals of between five and nine years, but after Cnut's reign more frequently, every three years or less.[9] Differences between the royal portraits and the designs on the reverse make it possible to distinguish types easily, and they are commonly identified by such names as Hand, Crux, Pointed Helmet or Quatrefoil[10] (Figure 1c). The evidence of hoards and mules (i.e. coins made with dies of different types) show that types were issued consecutively. There is no doubt

[7] Blackburn, 'Æthelred's coinage'; Jonsson, *The New Era*.

[8] Stewart, 'The English and Norman mints'.

[9] Id., 'Coinage and recoinage'.

[10] The numbering of types proposed by Stewart, 'A numeration', is often used. Both are used in Table 4.

Figure 1. Silver pennies a. Edgar (959–975), Reform type (*c.*973–975), Stamford mint, moneyer Æscman b. Æthelred II (978–1016), Crux type (*c.*991–997), Exeter mint, moneyer Ælfstan c. Cnut (1016–1035), Quatrefoil type (1016/17–*c.*1023), Lincoln mint, moneyer Æthelmær. © Fitzwilliam, Museum, Cambridge

that minting standards were closely controlled after 973 as they probably had been since the seventh century.[11]

The study of the coinage has mainly to be based on the coins themselves, for the documentary references, although illuminating, give no indication of the complexity of the system or the effectiveness of royal control over it. As the coins circulating in England were reminted from time to time, it is necessary to study those that were withdrawn from circulation by being lost or exported and that have been discovered in hoards or as loose finds in excavations or by metal detectors. The main evidence comes from the period 990 to 1051 because it was then that large numbers were removed from England as tribute or as the wages of Scandinavian warriors who served the English king. Over 51,000 Anglo-Saxon coins of that period have been found in Scandinavia.[12] These make it possible to investigate the coinage much more systematically in the first half of the eleventh century than in the second, when we depend almost entirely on the relatively few coins that have been found in England.

It is likely that the current type had to be used to pay taxes and other renders to the king, and in markets supervised by royal officials.[13] For such purposes, old coins had to be exchanged for the current type, and a fee paid to the moneyer. During the currency of a type, the weight was gradually reduced before being raised again when the next type was introduced. Mark Blackburn explains: 'This manipulation of the weight standard appears to have been a deliberate mechanism to encourage people to bring coin and bullion into the mint throughout the life of the issue. This would have been achieved by offering a better exchange rate, i.e. more coins to the pound of silver, towards the end of a coin type.'[14] Hoards show that the coins in circulation were normally of one or two consecutive

[11] Lyon, 'Some problems', 195–208, 216–17.
[12] Blackburn and Jonsson, 'The Anglo-Saxon and Anglo-Norman element'.
[13] Stewart, 'Coinage and recoinage', 467–8.
[14] Blackburn, 'Coinage', 115.

types, but older coins still had value, if not as much as the current type, and hoards of them can be compared to modern bank deposits. Several hoards of this kind deposited in the reign of Edward the Confessor (1042–1066) have been found, but earlier ones are rare, probably because old coins were used to pay the very large tributes or taxes that were exacted by Edward's predecessors.[15]

Surviving coins are not a reliable guide to the productivity of a mint.[16] The number of dies used to make them is a much better one; moneyers did not normally use more than they needed. Careful study of the surviving coins of a type show how many dies were used in each mint to make them. Recently, much attention has been paid to ways of estimating the total number of dies used in each mint to produce each type. These methods and the results they yield are discussed in the Appendix. They have made it possible to estimate the productivity of English mints in the late tenth and early eleventh centuries with more confidence than is normally possible. The results cast welcome light on the economy in the eleventh century. Christopher Dyer has objected that 'the real wealth of a country should be measured not by the amount of silver issued by its mints, but by its ability to produce sufficient goods to give its people an adequate living'.[17] There are, however, good reasons, discussed in Chapter 5, for thinking that most of the silver in England's abundant coinage in the century before the Norman Conquest came from Germany to pay for English produce, and that the productivity of the major mints on or near the east coast reflects the profitability of England's export trade. It is also worth emphasizing that the size of the currency was an important factor in England's prosperity. Numismatic evidence, in conjunction with that yielded by the Domesday enquiries, provides the starting point of this book.

---

[15] Blackburn, 'The Welbourne Hoard'; Lyon, 'Variations', 114–18.

[16] They are, however, used to rank eleventh-century towns in *CUHB*, 558–9 (Table 22.1) and 750–1 (Appendix 1B).

[17] Dyer, *Making a Living*, 70.

Domesday Book is the first detailed source of information about England's resources and their distribution. It was based on the results of enquiries made in 1086 throughout the kingdom. According to the contemporary *Anglo-Saxon Chronicle*, an account that has been largely confirmed by modern studies, it had two main purposes:[18] first, to review tax assessments and record what lands the king had and what dues he ought to have; and, secondly, to record the lands held by the 'archbishops, bishops, abbots, earls and what or how much everyone had who was occupying land in England, in land and cattle and how much money it was worth'.[19] For the purpose of these enquiries the shires were grouped in seven circuits, each supervised by a group of commissioners who gathered information from royal officials and landowners that was checked in shire courts and by local juries. Each circuit sent a return to Winchester, apparently by August 1086. Six of them were then edited and abbreviated (omitting details of demesne stock) to form a single text now known as Great Domesday Book (GDB) that was written by one scribe, with corrections by another. The return from the eastern circuit (Essex, Norfolk, and Suffolk) was not processed in this way but was kept together with GDB and is now known as Little Domesday Book (LDB).[20] Most of the return from the south-western circuit (Wiltshire, Dorset, Somerset, Devon, and Cornwall) has also survived and is known as *Liber Exoniensis* (Exon Domesday). There are about 30 other texts with additional information, known as Domesday Satellites, most of them later copies, that were submitted to the commissioners or compiled during the processing of the results of their enquiries.[21]

As the circuit commissioners did not all interpret their instructions in the same way, Ann Williams warns that 'when comparing

[18] Williams, 'Domesday Book'.

[19] *ASC s.a.* 1085.

[20] Roffe, *Domesday*, 222–3, argues that LDB was a first attempt to process a circuit return that served as 'the prototype that inspired GDB'.

[21] Clarke, 'Domesday satellites'.

region with region, it is important to distinguish real variations from by-products of the idiosyncrasies of the circuit commissioners'.[22] Failure to do so has had serious consequences. For example, in some circuits large estates were treated as units with little or no information about their component parts, while in some other circuits such estates were described in detail. This has badly affected discussions of the history of settlement.[23] More serious is the suspicion that such fundamental regional features as the manorial structure in the northern Danelaw and the unusually free element in the East Anglian peasantry were 'simply illusions created by the way in which Domesday Book was produced'.[24]

Some apparent regional differences were also created in the final stage of the production of Domesday Book.[25] A clear example is the treatment of the northern circuit (Yorkshire, Lincolnshire, Huntingdonshire, Nottinghamshire, and Derbyshire), the first to be processed. The work began with Yorkshire, Lincolnshire, and Huntingdonshire, in which no slaves were recorded. They began to be noted in Nottinghamshire and Derbyshire, and then in every other shire.[26]

Domesday Book is, consequently, not a reliable guide to many details of the economy. Fortunately the compilers did obey their instruction to record the cash value of all estates. Some are estimates, but most were real rents.[27] These confirm the numismatic evidence that there was a great deal of cash in circulation, an important factor in eleventh-century England's remarkable prosperity.[28]

---

[22] Williams, 'Domesday Book', 144.

[23] Sawyer, 'Early medieval English settlement', 2–4.

[24] Baxter, 'The representation of lordship', 79.

[25] Roffe, 'Domesday Book and northern society'; Sawyer and Thacker, 'The Cheshire Domesday', 294–5.

[26] Darby, *Domesday England*, 338.

[27] Lennard, *Rural England*, 105–28.

[28] Estimates of the number of coins in circulation in the eleventh century are discussed in the Appendix.

2

Tempore Regis Edwardi

The Domesday texts discussed in the previous chapter provide a great deal of information about agricultural resources and their exploitation twenty years after the Conquest.[1] They also note, less systematically, other resources including fish, salt, iron, and lead, but cast little light on the manufacture of cloth, pottery, leather goods, and other craft products that certainly made important contributions to English wealth.[2] With few exceptions the annual income from every manor was recorded, normally in terms of money, although there are some references to renders in kind. As most lords, apart from Norman and French monasteries, may have taken renders in kind from some of their manors, the money values are in part estimates of the worth of those renders.

It has recently been claimed that in the real world many lords obtained little or no cash from a manor, but took delivery of foodstuffs for consumption by the household.[3] That is probably true of those who had one or two manors, but not of major landowners, some of whom can be shown to have taken substantial amounts of

---

[1] Lennard, *Rural England*; Harvey, 'Domesday England'.
[2] Darby, *Domesday England*, 260–88.
[3] Dyer, *Making a Living*, 98.

cash as well as produce from their estates. The best documented example is Christ Church, Canterbury. Archbishop Lanfranc reorganized its manors so that twenty-six of them rendered both produce and money to feed the community and its servants, while thirteen rendered only money for clothing. Almost all the manors, including those that provided food-farms, also paid rent (*gablum*) and customary dues (*gersum*), totalling £101 and £115 respectively, in cash. The total cash income of the monastery was approximately £573.[4] The total valuation of its property in Domesday Book was £810, which means that the produce rendered was valued at £237. In other words, the cash income was worth twice as much as the produce.

The king and all his major tenants certainly required produce, especially from manors near their residences, but the same manors probably also rendered cash. Most major landowners also had distant manors that they never or rarely visited. The income from such manors was probably mostly in cash, although some especially valuable produce such as honey or iron was often reserved for the lord. This method of exploiting large and dispersed estates is most clearly seen in the descriptions of *Terra Regis*.[5] Edward the Confessor rarely ventured far from southern England,[6] and in his reign many of the royal manors there rendered provisions, described as farms for a number of days or nights. The fact that almost all the royal manors in Wiltshire, Dorset, and south Gloucestershire are not given a money value for 1086 suggests that they still supplied the king with produce.[7] In contrast, the main renders from royal manors in East Anglia and Essex are described as payments of coin by weight, tale, or assayed.[8]

[4] Canterbury Cathedral, Register K, fos. 69v–70; Lennard, *Rural England*, 120–1.

[5] Lennard, *Rural England*, 126–30; Stafford, 'The "Farm of One Night"'.

[6] Hill, *An Atlas*, 94.

[7] Darby, *Domesday England*, 357–8.

[8] That is, by counting, weighing or taking account of the silver content, measured by the method used in the twelfth-century Exchequer described in *Dialogus*, 36–9. For the interpretation of Domesday terminology, in particular the formula 'de xx in ora', see Lyon, 'Silver weight', 232–8.

Although some lords managed their own manors with the help of reeves, most delegated that task to lessees who paid rent, or to farmers: that is, individuals or groups who undertook to run the manor and pay an agreed 'farm'. The values recorded in Domesday Book were the incomes that lords obtained from their manors. In the many entries reporting that a manor rendered more than its value, the value was probably what was paid earlier, possibly before the Conquest, while the render was what the current lord demanded, which is sometimes described as too much.[9]

The Canterbury evidence shows that some of the values given in DB for Archbishop Lanfranc's manors included rents and customary dues additional to the farms, but that some did not. This means that the total income from his manors was more than the Domesday valuations.[10] It is not possible to assess the effect of such inconsistency, but the Lincolnshire Domesday suggests that many manorial incomes were substantially more than the Domesday values. A total of 267 entries record a render described as *tailla* in addition to the value. Stenton was probably right to explain it as money paid to the lord outside the sum for which the lessees of the manor answered to him.[11] It was normally a pound or less, but for several major manors it was very much more, sometimes exceeding the value. The total amounted to £610; the manorial values totalled £3253. As Lincolnshire was processed at an early stage in the compilation of DB, the omission of references to *tailla* elsewhere may have been the result of an 'editorial' decision. If so, the total of manorial incomes was substantially more than the £72,000 that Domesday records.[12]

Domesday Book normally records the main resources that contributed to manorial incomes. The most important were the peasants who were obliged to provide services of various kinds, the most

---

[9] Lennard, *Rural England*, 155–6.
[10] *The Domesday Monachorum*, 98–9; Lennard, *Rural England*, 203–6.
[11] Stenton, 'Introduction to the Lincolnshire Domesday', xxiii.
[12] Roffe, 'Domesday Book and northern society'.

burdensome being regular week-work, and also to pay rents and customary dues. A survey of the estates of Burton Abbey, made in or
soon after 1114, shows that the tenants included a large number of
censarii, who are not recorded in DB, and who owed small money
rents but not services.[13] A few *censarii* are recorded elsewhere in DB,
but the Burton survey suggests that many more may have been omitted. DB also carefully records the number of plough-teams (or
plough-oxen) belonging to both manorial demesnes and the peasants who were obliged to help cultivate the demesne arable. Other
manorial resources recorded in DB, if less consistently, were meadows, pasture, woodland, and mills. These were considered the property of the lord, although they were also used by peasants who paid
for the privilege in kind or cash.

DB enabled the king's agents to discover what the property held
by his tenants was worth, but it gives no information about the
amount or value of the produce retained by reeves, lessees or farmers, or by the peasants for their own consumption or sale. This means
that DB does not provide evidence for a comprehensive account of
the English economy. It does, however, make possible some reasonable, if approximate, estimates of such important economic factors
as the size of the population, and the extent of arable.

Attempts to determine the size of the population in 1086 have
been hampered by the fact that the only people it enumerates systematically are peasants whose renders in kind and services contributed to the value of the manors. There are almost 270,000 of them
and most must have had families. As later medieval evidence suggests that the average size of a rural household was five persons, the
recorded peasants represent about 1,350,000 people.[14] There are,
however, many omissions. The four northern shires are virtually

[13] Bridgeman, 'The Burton Abbey twelfth-century surveys'; Darby, *Domesday England*,
85–6, 340; Walmsley, 'The *Censarii* of Burton Abbey'.

[14] Moore, 'The Anglo-Norman family'.

excluded, and the account of Lancashire is incomplete. There were numerous monasteries and nunneries, but the only religious community whose members and servants are counted is Bury St Edmunds. There is no means of knowing how many tenants were omitted because, like the *censarii* of Burton Abbey, they only paid money rents. Other significant omissions are the households and servants of the tenants-in-chief and their tenants. Only sixty-eight reeves (*prepositi*) are mentioned but there were hundreds more, not all of whom were drawn from the peasants who were recorded. There were over 6000 mills but only six millers or mill keepers are listed. Other substantial omissions are indicated by the small numbers of brewers (40), cowmen (2), fishermen (92), foresters (4), potters (5), shepherds (10), and smiths (64).[15] There is only one huntsman and one carpenter. Christopher Dyer has recently concluded that, taking account of the incomplete description of towns, discussed below, a likely estimate of the total population in 1086 would lie somewhere between 2.2 and 2.5 million.[16]

The 81,118 plough teams make it possible to gain some idea of the extent of arable. Although in reality some plough-teams were larger or smaller than the conventional eight oxen team of DB, the total can be accepted as roughly correct. On the assumption that each team worked about 100 acres a year, over 8 million acres were cultivated. If the yield was the same as in the thirteenth century, the grain produced could have provided everyone in normal years with more than enough to sustain healthy life if combined with other foods.[17] Woodland was also a vital resource and was carefully recorded. Unfortunately, DB describes it in such varied ways that its total extent is uncertain.[18] The best estimate is about 4 million acres, which with

[15] Darby, *Domesday England*, 336–46.
[16] Dyer, *Making a Living*, 95.
[17] Ibid. 96.
[18] Darby, *Domesday England*, 171–87.

peat would have provided fuel for the whole population and abundant material for fencing and buildings.[19]

The only livestock, other than plough-oxen, that were systematically recorded by the surveyors were those belonging to manorial lords. That information was, however, omitted from GDB apart from a few incidental references, and is only preserved, with some omissions, for four eastern and four south-western counties. The manorial demesnes in those shires had 283,000 sheep, 48,000 pigs, 24,000 goats and 23,000 *animalia*, most of them cattle.[20] The numbers of other animals are so low that they cannot have been fully recorded.

There are, however, indications that the total number of livestock held by peasants was much greater than on the demesnes.[21] That was demonstrably true of plough-oxen. In five counties that were analysed by Baring (Berkshire, Buckingham, Hertford, Middlesex, and Surrey) there were 1530 demesne teams while the peasants had 5113.[22] The proportion between demesne and peasant teams varied greatly, but the overall ratio was probably approximately 1:3, as in the counties Baring studied.

In the thirteenth and fourteenth centuries there was a huge number of sheep producing wool, England's most valuable export. It is therefore worth considering how far sheep were a major source of England's wealth in the eleventh century.[23] Apart from a short period at the time of the Norman Conquest, the sheep bones found in the excavation of eleventh-century sites are generally of animals that were at least 3 years old, showing that they were reared for their wool and milk rather than meat, although mutton was welcome food and consumed in large quantities.[24] In a brief summary

[19] Dyer, *Making a Living*, 96.
[20] Darby, *Domesday England*, 164.
[21] Harvey, 'Domesday England', 46, 121–31, 136.
[22] Baring, *Domesday Tables*, 17, 51, 85, 107, 143.
[23] Lennard, *Rural England*, 260–4.
[24] O'Connor, *Animal Bones from Flaxengate*, 23–4, 48.

of the evidence, Terry O'Connor reports that most sheep remains were of animals that were 3 to 6 years old and argues that 'the relatively low population of old adults at most sites suggests that the production of wool was not the highest or exclusive priority'. He does, however, point out that 'the first two fleeces are likely to be the best quality that the sheep will produce'.[25] Their milk was used to make cheese; cheeses produced in Essex were unusually large and cost 6 pence each in the reign of Henry II.[26] Although documentary evidence is slight, there is enough to suggest that the number of sheep in the late eleventh century was not much smaller than two centuries later. A crude estimate of the total number of demesne sheep in 1086, based on the evidence for eight counties, is well over a million. A comparison of the demesne flocks recorded in Domesday with those on the same estates in later surveys suggests that there was no general increase in the size of demesne flocks in the twelfth and thirteenth centuries. For example, in Essex and Suffolk where St Paul's, London, had eight manors, on six of them the number of demesne sheep was almost the same or larger in Domesday than in 1222.[27] Similarly, on five manors of Christ Church, Canterbury, for which demesne flocks are recorded in 1086, the total number of sheep was 704, while in c.1322 there were only 620.[28] Ten of the fifteeen manors in Essex and East Anglia that were surveyed in the *Rotuli de Dominabus* of 1185 had fewer demesne sheep than in DB, although Henry II's surveyors reported that several could support many more.[29]

The only clues in DB indicating the total number of sheep are the many references in Norfolk and Suffolk to fold-soke (that is, the obligation to keep sheep on the manorial demesne to manure it), and to

[25] Id., 'Animal husbandry', 369, 371.
[26] Round, 'Introduction to the Essex Domesday', 373.
[27] Hale, *Domesday of St Paul's*, 122–39.
[28] Smith, *Canterbury Cathedral Priory*, 151–3.
[29] *Rotuli de dominabus*, 47–65.

the numbers of sheep that could be supported on the Essex marshes.[30] These suggest that the demesne flocks were a relatively small part of the total. This is confirmed by at least one entry describing Halvergate in Norfolk, where there were 260 demesne sheep, but 700 others that rendered 100 shillings.[31] The tax on movables of 1225 shows that in Wiltshire many tenants had numerous sheep, and that on the manors of Damerham and Martin in Hampshire 138 of the 207 tenants had 3850 sheep between them, while their lord, Glastonbury Abbey, had only 570. Similarly, at Tisbury in Wiltshire, Shaftesbury Abbey had 250 demesne sheep, but its tenants had 1333.[32]

In some areas Domesday records relatively high values per plough team. This was sometimes because profits of justice and other royal dues made a substantial contribution. In areas that were predominantly pastoral in the thirteenth and fourteenth centuries, the explanation is more likely to be that pastoral farming was already important in the eleventh century. Some specialized in dairy farming or rearing pigs, but much larger areas were renowned for their sheep. In discussing this possibility, Darby drew attention to three main problems that have to be faced when interpreting Domesday values.[33] The first is the great variety of ways in which values are expressed. Secondly, some values included, while others excluded, customary dues that were not part of the farm or rent. A third problem that particularly affects the mapping of values is the fact that the income of many manors, especially in the east and north, came partly from places that were distant from the manorial centre for which the value was given. Darby therefore excluded from his calculations those counties where the problems are most acute and concentrated on the area shown in Figure 2. For the rest of the country he was only able to use county totals, as in Figure 3. These show that

---

[30] Lennard, *Rural England*, 227, n. 2.
[31] LDB 128b–129a.
[32] Scott, 'Medieval agriculture', 26–9.
[33] Darby, *Domesday England*, 223–31.

ANNUAL VALUES

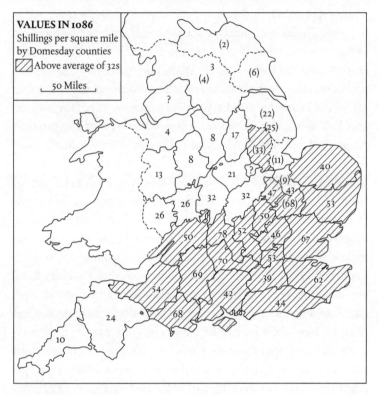

Figure 2. Distribution of annual values in 1086 (by Domesday counties). (From Darby, *Domesday England*, fig. 75, p. 228)

the part of England with a higher value per team than the average of 18 shillings extended from Somerset and Dorset in the west to Essex and Kent in the east, with a northern extension in Cambridgeshire. The most natural explanation for the high figure for Essex is that it reflects the extensive sheep pastures on the coastal marshes. The main concentrations of demesne sheep in Norfolk were on similar pastures along the north-east coast that extended into the Fens around the Wash. This also explains the high value per team in

ANNUAL VALUES

VALUES IN 1086
Shillings per team
by Domesday counties
Above average of 18s
50 Miles

Figure 3. Distribution of annual values per team (by Domesday counties). (From Darby, *Domesday England*, fig. 77, p. 230)

Cambridgeshire. It is significant that the chalklands of Dorset, Wiltshire, and Hampshire, where sheep farming was later very important, also have high values. Lincolnshire, where sheep farming was also important later, only has an overall value of 14 shillings per team, but in the main sheep areas it was much higher. In the southernmost wapentake Elloe, bordering Cambridgeshire and the Wash, it was 20 shillings, and with *tailla* 25 shillings. Similarly, Bolingbroke manor with its sokeland, between the Fens north-west of the Wash and the Wolds, was valued at £40 with £80 *tailla*; and the value per team was 26 shillings. This evidence strengthens the claim that in the eleventh century sheep were already an important source of England's wealth.[34]

The information provided by Domesday Book about conditions TRE is very slight, except for some towns. The only details regularly given for rural manors are the tax assessment, the name of the tenant, and the value. Nevertheless, taken together with the fuller account of the situation after 1066, it shows that on the eve of the Conquest England was more prosperous and its wealth was shared by many more people than 20 years later.

This was partly because the economy was badly disrupted by the Conquest, rebellions, and later invasions from Denmark, Ireland, and Scotland. Many areas had recovered by 1086, but in some there were still many manors that were waste or had greatly reduced values.[35] There were also natural disasters. The *Anglo-Saxon Chronicle* reports several years with exceptionally bad weather or murrain between 1042 and 1054, but none after that until 1070, followed by others in 1077, 1082, and 1086. It is possible that in the latter half of Edward's reign the Chronicler was more interested in the political conflicts, but if the record is more or less complete, it suggests that farming conditions in England were more favourable for several years before the Conquest than after it.

The Norman conquerors extracted a great deal more wealth from the English economy than their immediate predecessors, and earned the reputation of being greedy, even rapacious. The Anglo-Saxon

[34] In 'The wealth of England', 161–2, I suggested that the main market for English wool in the eleventh century was the nascent cloth industry of Flanders and Brabant. It has been objected that local supplies were more than adequate to sustain the industry at that time (Verhulst, *The Rise of Cities*, 136–7; Bolton, 'What is money?', 11). Nevertheless, the evidence reviewed here and on p. 105 shows that sheep were a valuable resource and that German merchants were buying wool in London, whatever its destination.

[35] Darby, *Domesday England*, 232–59.

Chronicler, commenting on William's reign in 1087, wrote: 'The king and his chief men loved gain much and over much—gold and silver—and did not care how sinfully it was obtained provided it came to them.' It is uncertain whether Edward reintroduced the geld after it was dropped in 1051,[36] but under William it was once again an annual tax. The normal rate was probably 2 shillings per hide, or carucate as it was in the early twelfth century, but in 1084 and possibly 1086 the rate was trebled. The collectors then reported many failures to pay.[37] Many of the king's tenants obtained substantial reductions in the assessment of their lands, and some of their demesne manors were completely exempted. That did not reduce the burden on their peasants, for some, probably most, lords continued to collect the geld and retain it.[38]

Despite the disruption of many towns, William exacted a great deal more from them than Edward did.[39] The demesne manors of the king and some of his chief men were also made to yield much more than they did before the Conquest. This was rarely the result of increased productivity; most lords necessarily had to rely on English reeves as their predecessors had done. Manorial incomes were increased by the exercise of power; by raising rents, demanding cash payments from peasants for their traditional rights to use pasture, meadows, and woodland, or by reducing the status of peasants who had been relatively privileged and imposing greater burdens on them.[40] Even in Shropshire, where the total value dropped from £925 to £861 and many manors had been wasted since the Conquest, the value of a few held by Earl Roger and others had increased.[41] Most

[36] Barlow, *Edward the Confessor*, 106n, 155–7.

[37] Round, 'Danegeld', 87–9; Galbraith, *Making of DB*, 87–101; Welldon Finn, *Domesday Studies: Liber Exoniensis*, 105–8.

[38] Harvey, 'Taxation and the economy', 257–62.

[39] See below, n. 52.

[40] Johnson, 'Introduction to the Norfolk Domesday', 30; Harvey, 'Domesday England', 64, 73, 92–3.

[41] Tait, 'Introduction to the Shropshire Domesday', 281.

bishops and religious communities were less successful. Archbishop Lanfranc was the main exception. He raised the value of his manors, including those he recovered, from about £800 a year to about £1200. A record of the income from his demesne manors gives the total value of his farms as about £1250 with, in addition, rents and customary dues totalling £210.[42] He also greatly increased the revenues of his cathedral monastery and the bishopric of Rochester.

Most lay landowners were not able to increase the value of their manors so dramatically, but the Lincolnshire evidence of *tailla* discussed above suggests that many lords obtained some income in addition to the Domesday values. This evidence justifies the claim that England was far more prosperous and that many freemen, sokemen, and other relatively free peasants had more cash to spend on the eve of the Conquest than after 20 years of Norman rule.

The Normans exported large amounts of cash and treasure. After his coronation William ostentatiously paraded his newly won wealth on a triumphal progress through Normandy and throughout his reign he used English wealth to maintain his authority in Normandy and to defend his continental empire.[43] Not all those who acquired large estates after the Conquest broke links with their homelands. William remained duke of Normandy, spent much of his time there, and was buried in Caen. His churches there owed much to the wealth of England.[44] Several of his leading barons did likewise; William de Warenne, Roger de Beaumont, and Roger de Montgomery retained extensive estates in Normandy.[45] The first generation of conquerors established very few religious houses in England and continued to regard the family foundations across the Channel with special favour, endowing them with English estates and churches.[46] Cash was also

---

[42] *The Domesday Monachorum*, 98–9.
[43] Douglas, *William the Conqueror*, 208–9.
[44] Musset, 'Les conditions financières'.
[45] Le Patourel, *Norman Barons*.
[46] Matthew, *The Norman Monasteries*, 26–65.

used to pay mercenaries recruited for the initial Conquest and again in 1085 when the Danish king Knut, in alliance with the king of Norway and the duke of Flanders, planned to conquer England.[47] William took the threat very seriously and returned from Normandy in the autumn 'with a larger force of mounted men and infantry from France and Brittany than had ever come to this country, so that people wondered how this country could maintain all that army.'[48] The invasion was never launched, and when the foreign warriors returned home they must have been well paid in cash. Treasure was also removed by raiders, and by English lords who went into exile.

The fact that William and his chief men were able to extort a great deal more cash than their predecessors shows that the economy was not crippled, although in the long run they and their successors harmed it.[49] The post-Conquest buoyancy of the economy was not due to the Normans; it was built on foundations laid before 1066.

Our knowledge of towns in the middle of the eleventh century depends on DB, supplemented by archaeological and numismatic evidence.[50] They were surveyed in 1086 mainly in order to discover what dues the king ought to have from them. Over 100 are described but the amount of detail varies greatly. For some it gives only the value, but for others it records the number of tenements in 1086 and how many had been lost to make room for castles or other buildings, or were waste because of such misfortunes as poverty, burdensome taxes, fire or the abuse of power by sheriffs or magnates. Such detailed information is given for several of the largest towns, but folios left blank for London and Winchester were not used. Fortunately there are two early surveys of Winchester, one of the king's

[47] Prestwich, 'War and finance'; Lund, *Lið, leding og landeværn*, 187–208.

[48] *ASC s. a.* 1085.

[49] Harvey, 'Taxation and the economy'.

[50] Tait, *Medieval English Borough*, Darby, *Domesday England*, 289–320, 364–8; Reynolds, 'Towns in DB'; Biddle, 'Towns'.

part made c.1110 revising one made c.1057, and one of the whole town in 1148.[51]

Despite the disruption, William extracted a great deal more from most towns than Edward did. For example, Rochester's render rose from £5 a year TRE to £40 in 1086, while Lincoln's rose from £30 to £100 with an additional £75 for the mint. In 1086 the total rendered by towns annually was well over £2000.[52] The implication is that towns-people retained much more of their earnings TRE than in 1086. Many English towns were flourishing before the Conquest, and some had expanding suburbs.[53] Most were small, but at least twenty-one had more than 200 burgesses before the Conquest,[54] and at least six had more than 1000 tenements or burgesses.[55] An estimate that Winchester had about 1130 tenements TRE is based on comparison of the two early surveys.[56] London was certainly larger than York.[57]

Estimating the population of towns on the basis of such information must involve much guesswork.[58] Apart from 'the horrible problem of multipliers',[59] some tenements were larger than others and some were unoccupied, but some, perhaps many, tenements had several houses.[60] Burgesses and their families were not the only inhabitants. There were servants, apprentices, labourers, and carters,

[51] Barlow, 'The Winton Domesday', 9–10, 18–19.

[52] Tait, *Medieval English Borough*, 183-5. The recorded total was over £1800, but that does not include London or Winchester. For the increased yield of mints, see Grierson, 'Domesday Book, The geld *De Moneta*'; Metcalf, 'The taxation of moneyers'.

[53] E.g. Lincoln: Sawyer, *Anglo-Saxon Lincolnshire*, 184–5; Norwich: Carter, 'Anglo-Saxon origins'; Winchester: Biddle, 'Early Norman Winchester', 323; cf. Darby, *Domesday England*, 293.

[54] Tait, *Medieval English Borough*, 130.

[55] York: c.1875, Maxwell, 'Yorkshire: the East Riding', 154; Norwich: 1320, LDB 116a; Lincoln; 1272, Roffe, Introduction to the Lincolnshire Domesday; Oxford: 1032, Blair, *Anglo-Saxon Oxfordshire*, 155–9.

[56] Biddle and Keene, *Winchester*, 468.

[57] Keene, 'Medieval London', 107.

[58] Holt, 'Society and population', 82–3.

[59] Reynolds, 'Towns in DB', 305.

[60] Biddle and Keene, *Winchester*, 343–4, 440–1; Sawyer, *Anglo-Saxon Lincolnshire*, 190.

as well as clergy and royal officials. Cottagers are sometimes recorded as living in towns, or near enough to be considered part of the urban community.[61] Some of the bordars noted in 1086, for example the 480 in Norwich who were too poor to pay custom, may have been former burgesses,[62] but there must have been many poor people who were not. Dunwich in Suffolk is a most revealing case. Despite the erosion of much of its territory by the sea, the number of burgesses had increased from 120 to 236 in 1086, when there were also 178 poor men.[63] Such men, normally ignored in Domesday because they contributed nothing to the king's revenue, were probably to be found in most towns before the Conquest as well as after. It does therefore seem reasonable to assume that estimates of urban populations based on the assumption that each tenement or burgess represented a household of five people are far too low, although we cannot hope to know by how much.[64]

Most towns needed more food than they could produce; they also needed wood or peat for fuel, timber for building, and raw materials for craftsmen. Supplies came from the surrounding countryside, but they could also be brought from distant sources. At the beginning of the century London was already importing food, wine, cloth, and much else from many places between Normandy and the Rhineland,[65] and there is reason to think that dried cod, an important form of preserved food, was already being imported from northern Norway in the eleventh century, as it was later.[66] In return, urban workshops supplied the rural population with pottery, clothing, brooches, footwear, combs, tools, and other goods. There were several means of

---

[61] Dyer, 'Towns and cottages'.

[62] LDB 119a; Reynolds, 'Towns in DB', 306n.

[63] LDB 311b.

[64] Reynolds, 'Towns in DB', 305–6.

[65] IV Atr 2–3.

[66] Sawyer, *Anglo-Saxon Lincolnshire*, 182–3; id., 'Early development of towns', 36–7. See below', pp. 96–7.

distribution ranging from pedlars to contractors, who supplied large quantities of goods, but the markets that were an essential feature of all towns were the most important. DB notes only nineteen urban markets and their renders; the dues of others must have been included in the total town renders.[67] There were also many rural markets, most of them probably held on Sundays in or near churchyards.[68] DB records 40 in 1086 and gives the value of most of them.[69] A few are described as new, but most were long established and there were many more that were probably omitted because their dues were included in manorial values. It is, however, likely that many rendered nothing TRE. This is suggested by the evidence from Lincolnshire that some Norman lords began to take tolls in havens or at ferries that had never happened before the Conquest.[70]

There was also a lively overseas trade in basic goods as well as luxuries.[71] The evidence of the coinage shows that in the eleventh century English exports were on a much larger scale than has generally been recognized. It suggests that Henry of Huntingdon's description of Anglo-German trade in the 1140s was also true a century earlier. According to Henry, 'although little silver was mined in England, much was brought from Germany by the Rhine on account of England's wonderful fertility in fish and meat, in most precious wool, and in cattle without number. As a result, a larger supply of silver is found in England than in Germany.'[72]

The silver produced in England came from lead-ores, but as their average silver content was low they could not yield large quantities.[73] The Romans extracted lead in South Wales, the Mendips, Shropshire,

---

[67] Darby, *Domesday England*, 318.
[68] Sawyer, 'Early fairs and markets'.
[69] Darby, *Domesday England*, 369–70.
[70] Sawyer, *Anglo-Saxon Lincolnshire*, 21.
[71] See Chapter 5.
[72] Henry of Huntingdon, *Historia Anglorum*, 5–6.
[73] Tylecote, *Metallurgy*, 73–9. See below, p. 33; the claim that Britain was a major source of silver in the Roman Empire is mistaken.

Derbyshire, and elsewhere, but the only lead production recorded in DB was in Derbyshire where five royal manors are reported to have jointly rendered 40 pounds of pure silver in 1086.[74] Lennard recognized that lead was probably mined elsewhere in 1086 but commented that 'in view of the silence of Domesday we can hardly suppose that it was on a sufficient scale to make much difference to the pattern of economic life even in the immediate neighbourhood of the mines'.[75] It is significant that the nearest mint to the Derbyshire lead workings used very few dies.[76]

John Maddicott has suggested that Alston Moor in Cumberland, where the Romans may have extracted silver, was a significant source of the metal in the seventh and eighth centuries.[77] His claim that in the twelfth century it was temporarily 'Europe's main silver producing centre' greatly exaggerates its importance. The Alston mines were leased for up to 500 marks a year in the 1160s but their output then declined rapidly.[78] Although silver production in the Harz mountains diminished rapidly after 1040, a little continued near Goslar and by 1168 a vastly richer source, soon called Freiberg, had been discovered near Meissen, on the Elbe.[79]

Domesday Book and other eleventh-century texts show that, although many renders were in kind, coins were used for many transactions, large and small. Numismatic evidence confirms that England then had a large and well-controlled coinage. It was, however, produced and managed for the purposes of government, not commerce. Coins manifested royal authority and were used by kings to make gifts, pay soldiers, and reward servants. They also facilitated

---

[74] GDB 272v; cf. Darby, *Domesday England*, 268–9.

[75] Lennard, *Rural England*, 241–2.

[76] Metcalf, 'Continuity and change', 2, 82–3.

[77] Maddicott, 'Two frontier states', 31–2.

[78] Poole, *From Domesday Book to Magna Carta*, 82. See now Allen, 'Silver production and the money supply', 115–18. This detailed discussion of the possible sources of silver in England and Wales after 1086 confirms the importance of imported silver.

[79] Spufford, *Money and its Use*, 95–6, 112–14.

the collection of taxes, royal dues, and legal penalties. Recoinages were a source of revenue and enabled royal agents to control the quality of the coins. Weight changes between and during types also contributed to the king's revenue, but by how much and in what ways is still obscure.[80] In a detailed discussion of the metrology of late Anglo-Saxon coins, Stewart Lyon comments 'that the monetary policy of late Anglo-Saxon England was highly sophisticated and subject to effective central direction, but with sufficient flexibility to tolerate both local and national variations in metrology without causing the system to break down'.[81]

The number of coins produced from time to time was partly determined by the needs of the government, for example to collect taxes or pay tributes. Payments to Scandinavian raiders or mercenaries explain the very large numbers minted between 990 and 1042. The size of a mintage was also limited by the amount of silver available. The main sources were English coins, in circulation or hoarded, foreign coins and bullion imported by merchants, and treasures held by churches or laymen that could be used to meet exceptional demands such as those made by Cnut and William as conquerors. The stock was reduced by exports as gifts, by traders or raiders, or by the wages of foreigners serving the English king. After the Norman Conquest there were also large transfers to Normandy and elsewhere on the Continent by William and his men.[82] After the coinage reform of c.973 almost all the silver needed to replace losses came ultimately from German mines.[83]

The reserves of treasure were greatly reduced by Cnut's demands but they soon recovered. The hoards deposited in Edward's reign and during William's campaigns between 1066 and 1070 contain large

[80] Lyon, 'Variations'; id., 'Some problems'; Petersson, 'Coins and weights'; Metcalf, An Atlas, 56–69.

[81] Lyon, 'Some problems', 208.

[82] Above, pp. 22–3.

[83] See Chapter 5.

numbers of obsolete coins, and on the eve of the Conquest large quantities of treasure were held by some magnates and by many churches and monasteries. Very little has survived, but in the eleventh century many churches compiled lists of their treasures. Some were made to record the names of donors. Others were produced after losses had occurred or were threatened. Exeter Cathedral kept a list of the gifts it received from Bishop Leofric (1046–1072).[84] William of Malmesbury was able to give some information about gifts to Glastonbury and the loss of some of them. He reported that Brihtwold, bishop of Ramsbury (1005–1045) gave his old community two chalices, one of them made of 20 marks of silver and 4 marks of gold, 'the other of less weight but greater value', gospels, a censer, an altar and 25 crosses, adding that two of them raised 22 gold marks (£132) when Abbot Æthelnoth (1053–1077/8) plundered them.[85]

Treasure figures prominently in accounts of the aristocratic and royal politics of the eleventh century. Descriptions of treasure in these texts may often be literary inventions rather than literally true, but they do demonstrate that the display of treasure was a powerful symbol in the real world. A lost passage from the *Vita Ædwardi* that has been recognized in a fourteenth-century work by Richard of Cirencester records gifts made by Godwin's daughter as queen to King Edward:

> Edith, from the very beginning of her marriage, clad him in raiments either embroidered by herself or of her choice, and of such a kind that it could not be thought that even Solomon in all his glory was ever thus arrayed. In the ornamentation of these no count was made of the cost of the precious stones, rare gems and shining pearls that were used. As regards mantles, tunics, boots and shoes, the amount of gold which flowed in the various complicated floral designs was not weighed. The throne, adorned with coverings embroidered with gold, gleamed in

---

[84] Robertson, *Anglo-Saxon Charters*, 226–31.
[85] Scott, *The Early History of Glastonbury*, 138–9.

every part; the floors were strewn with precious carpets from Spain. Edward's staff, for everyday use when walking, was encrusted with gold and gems. His saddle and horse-trappings were hung with little beasts and birds made from gold by smiths under her direction.[86]

Her family were exceptionally wealthy, but there are many indications that the eleventh-century aristocracy were no poorer than their tenth-century predecessors. Godgifu gave a silver necklace worth 100 marks to Coventry, and Tofig the Proud with his wife adorned the Holy Rood of Waltham with silver plate, a gold crown with gems, a gold footrest made of necklaces and bracelets, and a gold girdle set with gems made from her headband.[87]

Much lay treasure was acquired in this way by churches. The character of the treasure that could be accumulated by a great church is well illustrated by Ely. Three inventories made between 1075 and 1145 are preserved in the *Liber Eliensis*, which also contains numerous references to specific gifts and losses.[88] It is possible to identify many items that were at Ely in 1065. The earliest list was made after the monks had been forced to use many treasures from the church to raise the 1000 marks needed to secure William's peace. Much remained: 26 or 27 chalices, large and small, most of them of silver or silver gilt and the largest weighing almost 15 pounds (one gold one was lighter but worth more), 27 crosses, mostly silver gilt, and some with gold and figures in ivory or gold with gems, 2 silver candelabra, 3 censers, altars, hangings, and 13 reliquaries as well as elaborate shrines of Æthelthryth and her companions. There were also 283 books including at least 12 gospels with elaborate covers and many vestments; the earliest list has 38 copes, 40 chasubles, and 19

---

[86] Barlow, *The Life of King Edward*, 22–5; Tyler, 'When wings incarnadine with gold'.

[87] Dodwell, *Anglo-Saxon Art*, 25, 119; Rogers, 'The Waltham Abbey relic-list'.

[88] *Liber Eliensis*, 196–7, 223–4. 288–94. I am indebted to Simon Keynes for allowing me to use, in advance of publication, the study of the Ely treasures that he is preparing with Alan Kennedy.

stoles—165 items in all. The gospels are carefully described in the third list. One copy, given by King Edgar, had 'a golden cross on the front, with Christ in majesty, four angels and the twelve apostles in silver, the whole surface was of gold with precious and enamelled stones. The other side is of silver with figures of virgins'.

There is, therefore, good evidence that on the eve of the Norman Conquest there were some large stores of treasure, and a relatively large quantity of silver in circulation as coin. There were many poor, but there were also many people with cash to pay rent and tax, and some left to buy the produce of craftsmen. This had to be earned by selling produce or labour, implying active markets, urban and rural. This does not mean that England then had a money economy, but it certainly had a great deal of coin in circulation.[89]

The abundant coinage of eleventh-century England was a crucially important factor in its economic vitality. In the fifth century, when there was no coinage, the economy was based on barter, gift-giving, and the exaction of tribute by lords and overlords. The next three chapters are an attempt to trace and explain the development from that natural economy into the relatively urbanized and monetized economy TRE revealed by Domesday Book.

[89] See Appendix.

3

From Solidi to Sceattas

According to the geographer Strabo, before the Roman conquest Britain exported 'grain, cattle, gold, silver, hides, slaves and hunting dogs' and imported ivory, amber, and glass vessels. He also reported that the Britons bartered tin, lead, and hides in exchange for pottery, salt, and copper vessels.[1] There is no reason to doubt that Britain continued to export the same things when it was ruled by Rome, although little gold was produced after the second century and far more silver was imported than exported. The first and, as far as is known, only gold mine in Britain before the sixteenth century was begun soon after the Roman conquest in south-west Wales at Dolaucothi.[2] Extensive remains suggest that it was very productive for a while. It was probably this mine that encouraged Tacitus in AD 98 to write: 'Britain yields gold, silver, and other metals, to make it worth conquering.'[3] After it was abandoned, well before the end of Roman rule, surface gold may occasionally have been used but it was no longer a significant export; Bede did not include it in his list of

---

[1] Strabo, *Geography*, 157, 255, 259. For this chapter in general, see also Salway, *Roman Britain*.

[2] Burnham, *Dolaucothi-Pumsaint*.

[3] Tacitus, *Agricola*, ch. 12.

British produce.[4] He did, however, claim that Britain had rich veins of lead and silver.

The Romans certainly obtained large quantities of lead in Britain and there is no doubt that they extracted some silver.[5] At that time, and long afterwards, lead ores were the main source of silver in Britain, but as British ores have a low average silver content it is unlikely that they yielded substantial quantities; the Romans had much richer sources in other parts of their empire.[6] It has been claimed that as many more fourth-century silver coins have been found in Britain than elsewhere in the empire, Britain must have been an important source of silver.[7] A better explanation, discussed below, is that many more treasure hoards of the late fourth and early fifth centuries have been found in Britain than on the Continent.[8]

In the fourth century there was an abundance of gold and silver in the empire. The confiscation of the treasures of pagan temples by Constantine greatly increased the amount of bullion available and enabled him not only to richly endow churches but also to issue huge quantities of gold and silver coins.[9] He introduced the solidus of almost pure gold weighing about 4.5 g. At the end of the century, the normal gold coinage consisted of three denominations: the solidus; its half, the semis or semissis; and its third, the triens or tremissis, which became the main unit of coinage in western Europe in the sixth and seventh centuries. During the fourth century, and long afterwards, the imperial government maintained the quality of this gold coinage, but was less successful with the silver coinage.

---

[4] HE i.1; Tylecote, Metallurgy, 2–7.

[5] Frere, Britannia, 283–6.

[6] Tylecote, Metallurgy, 73–93. It is therefore unlikely that silver was an important export to the Byzantine Empire, as suggested by E. Campbell, Continental and Mediterranean Imports, 118, 138.

[7] Sutherland, Coinage and Currency, 90–2; Kent, 'From Roman Britain', 2.

[8] Martin, 'Wealth and treasure', 53–6, 65; Guest, Late Roman Gold and Silver, 29.

[9] This and the next two paragraphs are mainly based on Jones, The Later Roman Empire, 107–8, 438–40, and MEC, 6–12.

The weight of the most common denomination, generally known as a siliqua, was unstable and at the end of the century was at most 2 g and often less. There was, however, an abundance of silver plate, and in the fifth century, when only small quantities of silver coins were struck, mainly for ceremonial purposes, many payments were made in silver by weight. The explanation is, apparently, that the mint price of silver was less than the market price. In the fourth century there were also various denominations of bronze coins. Their main purpose was to redeem gold paid to officials and soldiers, but they also provided small change and were widely used in trading.[10] Such huge quantities were produced that their value dropped dramatically, and after 395 only one denomination was issued, a small coin that was called simply a *nummus* 'coin'. Sixty years later a solidus was valued at about 7000 nummi, but the rate fluctuated greatly and nummi were sometimes worth much less.

Very large numbers of gold coins circulated in the Empire in the fourth century. The annual income of the richest senators in the western Empire from their vast estates was up to 4000 lb (that is, about 1300 kg) of gold as well as a great deal of produce, and the income of senators of middle rank was from 1000 to 1500 lb of gold.[11] Many coins were also paid to soldiers. By the early fifth century the annual ration allowance of a soldier and his pay amounted to 5 solidi.[12] Although it is difficult to obtain reliable estimates of the size of the army from time to time, it is likely that in the early fifth century there were at least 100,000 soldiers serving in the field armies and frontier forces in the western Empire. If all received a minimum of 5 solidi a year, 7000 lb of gold was dispersed in this way in the western Empire annually.[13] The number of regular troops

---

[10] Kent, 'Gold coinage in the late Roman Empire'.
[11] Jones, *The Later Roman Empire*, 554–7. Amounts of gold in this paragraph are in Roman gold pounds that weighed 325 g.
[12] Ibid., 462.
[13] Ibid., 679–84.

was greatly reduced after 400, but large payments were then made to the leaders of invading armies. In 407 Alaric and his Visigoths demanded, and got, 4000 lb of gold, and later the Senate in Rome paid him 5000 lb of gold, 30,000 lb of silver, and goods including 3000 lb of pepper, but that did not prevent him sacking Rome in 410. Between 430 and 450 Theodosius II paid over 120,000 lb of gold to the Huns.[14]

Under the Romans, Britain imported a great variety of produce from many parts of the Empire and beyond its frontiers to supply the wants of imperial officials, the army, and people of high rank, many of whom were native Britons who adopted the customs and trappings of Roman civilization.[15] Some imports and exports were shipped by private traders, but far more were handled by agents of the government or of wealthy landowners.[16] Many valuable things also reached Britain by gift-exchange, a custom that was widespread in late Roman society from the emperor downwards.[17] A great deal of gold was needed to pay officials and soldiers, make political or diplomatic gifts, and for other purposes of the state. Above all, huge quantities of solidi were needed to pay soldiers.

The wealth accumulated in Roman Britain attracted raiders from others parts of the British Isles and from across the North Sea. The imperial government made great efforts to counter these threats by sending reinforcements when necessary, improving fortifications, and developing ports to facilitate the movement of troops and supplies across the Channel.[18] Britain was well worth defending. A panegyric on Constantius in 297, after he crushed a serious rebellion, described Britain as 'a land that the state could ill afford to lose, so plentiful are its harvests, so numerous are the pasturelands in which

[14] Ibid.,186; MEC, 9.
[15] Frere, Britannia, ch. 13.
[16] Jones, The Later Roman Empire, ch. 12.
[17] Wood, 'The exchange of gifts'.
[18] Frere, Britannia, 345–59; Wood, 'The Channel'.

it rejoices…so much wealth comes from its taxes'.[19] In the fourth century it was an important source of corn and other supplies for the army on the Rhine frontier. In 359 Julian, preparing for a major campaign across the Rhine, enlarged the fleet that shipped corn from Britain by having 400 ships built in less than 10 months.[20]

In the early fourth century, Roman Britain enjoyed several decades of prosperity. Many villas were rebuilt on a larger and more elaborate scale and the pottery industry flourished.[21] In the second half of the century, there were numerous attacks by its traditional enemies, then known as the Picts, who lived north of the Forth and Clyde estuaries, and the western coasts were raided by Scots and Attacotti. The main aim of these attacks was to gather plunder rather than win territory. As a result many Britons were enslaved and large quantities of treasure were seized.[22] Raids were reported in 360 and 365, and in 367 there was a major invasion by all three groups that overwhelmed the defences and caused a breakdown of military discipline. There was also widespread disorder that can reasonably be described as civil war.[23] It took the Roman commander Count Theodosius, father of the emperor Theodosius I, over a year to restore order. According to Ammianus Marcellinus he crossed the Channel with a powerful force from Boulogne to Richborough and marched to London.

> There he divided his troops into many parts and attacked the predatory bands of the enemy, which were ranging about and were laden with heavy burdens; quickly routing those who were driving along prisoners and cattle, he wrested from them the booty which the wretched tribute paying people had lost. And when all this had been restored to

---

[19] Cited by Maddicott, 'Prosperity and power', 50.
[20] Frere, *Britannia*, 350.
[21] Ibid., 292–3, 346.
[22] Pelteret, 'Slave raiding', 100–2, Maddicott, 'Frontier states', 34–5.
[23] Thompson, 'Ammianus Marcellinus and Britain'.

them, except for a small part which was allotted to the weary soldiers, he entered the city.[24]

He reorganized and strengthened Britain's defences and for over a decade they proved effective.

In 383 invading Picts and Scots were defeated by Magnus Maximus after he had been proclaimed Augustus by the army in Britain.[25] Maximus then crossed to Gaul with some of the best troops in an unsuccessful attempt to make good his claim. These troops did not return after he was executed in 388. Britain was then being raided not only by Picts and Scots, but also by Saxons.[26] The army was reinforced in 396, but the situation in the western Empire rapidly deteriorated and in 401 a legion was withdrawn. Early in 407 a usurping emperor, proclaimed by the army in Britain, who called himself Constantine III, crossed to Gaul with the remaining effective troops to combat a large force of barbarians who had crossed the frozen Rhine. He was successful for a while, but was executed in 411 on the orders of the legitimate emperor, Honorius. By then the Britons had expelled the Roman officials who remained and began to govern themselves. There were some rapid changes in the first decade of the fifth century. The large-scale industrial production of pottery ended abruptly, and imperial mints stopped sending coins to Britain.[27] The last bulk shipment of bronze coins was in 402 and the official supply of gold and silver coins probably ended before Constantine's usurpation. If so, this would help explain the discontent of the army that led it to proclaim and kill in quick succession two usurpers in 406. Constantine III was able pay his troops with solidi minted in his name in Gaul.

The history of Britain in the next two centuries is exceedingly obscure. Very different interpretations of the meagre evidence (much

---

[24] Casey, 'Magnus Maximus', 73.
[25] Chronicle of 452, trans. Murray, *From Roman to Merovingian Gaul*, 77.
[26] Wood, 'The Channel'.
[27] Fulford, 'Pottery production and trade'; Kent, 'From Roman Britain'.

of it archaeological) have been offered.[28] The main British text, the Ruin of Britain (*De Excidio Britanniae*) by Gildas, a well-educated British deacon, is a passionate call to kings and priests to reform, beginning with a brief account of episodes in British history that underline his message, with only vague indications of the date and location of events.[29] It has generally been accepted that it was written in the mid-sixth century, but Ian Wood has made a strong case for thinking that it was written between 475 and the 520s.[30] The only other texts written (or dictated) by a Briton in the fifth century are Patrick's *Letter to Coroticus*, a British king, and his *Confession*, composed late in his life.[31] They cast valuable light on the church in fifth-century Britain and on contacts between Ireland and Gaul.[32] The *Letter*, dated 470–471 by Charles Thomas, condemns Coroticus for enslaving Irish Christians and selling them to the pagan *Scotti*, who had presumably settled in western Scotland, and the Picts. In the *Confession* (chs. 10 and 62) he describes his capture and enslavement by Irish raiders when he was young, probably living near Carlisle.

Texts written on the Continent in the fifth and sixth centuries occasionally refer to Britain. This evidence has been carefully discussed by Ian Wood, whose conclusions are accepted in the brief account of the beginning of Anglo-Saxon England offered below. Archaeology casts light on many topics for which, in this period, texts provide little or no information; for example, the progress of Anglo-Saxon settlement, the fate of towns, and material culture.

[28] For example, cf. Wood, 'The end of Roman Britain', with Charles-Edwards, 'Nations and kingdoms', 24–30.

[29] *Gildas*.

[30] Wood, 'The end of Roman Britain', 22–3, confirmed by George, *Gildas*, 130, who opts for a date between *c*.480 and *c*.530, with a preference for the more limited *c*.510 and *c*.530; cf. Stenton, *Anglo-Saxon England*, 2, 'a little before the year 547'; Campbell, *The Anglo-Saxons*, 20, 'about 550'; Miller, 'Relative and absolute publication dates', '534x549'.

[31] *St Patrick: His Writings*.

[32] Thomas, 'Saint Patrick and fifth-century Britain'.

The cessation of regular coin imports after 410 means that they no longer provide reliable clues to the date of graves and other material remains, but increasingly sophisticated dating methods compensate for that loss.

Although large amounts of treasure must have been removed from Roman Britain by raiders, soldiers, and others who left in the last years of Roman rule, treasure hoards buried in the late fourth and early fifth centuries show that some, perhaps a great deal, remained to fuel internal conflicts and attract raiders. Since 1800 more than 100 hoards of late Roman gold and silver objects, many of them with coins struck between 395 and 402, have been found in Britain.[33] Many others must have been discovered earlier, but are not recorded. The fact that Roman coins, mostly of the fourth century, served for centuries as prototypes for Anglo-Saxon coins confirms that they were found from time to time in hoards or singly before the eleventh century, as they still are nowadays.[34]

In 1992 when a large hoard was found at Hoxne, Suffolk, it was quickly and skilfully excavated to be studied in detail in the British Museum.[35] The contents, which had been carefully packed in a wooden chest, included twenty-nine pieces of high-quality jewellery of very pure gold and over 100 items of small silver table-ware and toiletry, some with Christian symbols. It also contained 580 solidi struck between AD 364 and 405, 14,630 silver coins, all but one minted between AD 355 and 408, and twenty-four bronze coins. It was probably buried two or three decades after 408, by 450 at the latest.

In his detailed discussion of the Hoxne hoard, Guest argues that the abundance of early fifth-century treasure hoards in Britain

---

[33] Archer, 'Late Roman gold and silver hoards'. Guest, 'Hoards from the end of Roman Britain'.

[34] MEC, 158, Webster and Backhouse, *Making of England*, 105–6.

[35] Bland and Johns, *The Hoxne Treasure*; Guest, *The Late Roman Gold and Silver Coins from the Hoxne Treasure*.

cannot have been caused simply by the disruption following the end of Roman rule. Other parts of the western Empire were also disrupted at that time but have yielded far fewer hoards; the contrast between the 78 that were deposited between 395 and 411 in Britain and three from the same period in Italy is particularly striking.[36] He suggests that the population in certain areas of Britain buried hoards fully intending to leave them in the ground.

> The practice of burying but not recovering hoards of precious metals and Roman coins may have been directly related to the Romano-British population finding itself not only beyond the legal administration and military protection of the empire, but also outside the empire-wide elite exchange networks of gold and silver which, therefore, ceased to be of continued social value and were hence discarded.[37]

It is, however, more likely that many more hoards have been found in Britain than elsewhere in the empire because many wealthy Romans who left Britain expected to return. The fact that many objects in the Hoxne hoard were carefully packed suggests that it was hoped they would be recovered.

Some 98.5 per cent of the siliquae in the Hoxne hoard were clipped and filed round the edge, some of them very heavily. Similar clipped siliquae have been found in almost all British hoards of the late fourth and early fifth centuries, but are relatively rare in continental hoards. Guest states that there is now a consensus that clipping was a 'deliberate, almost certainly semi-official practice that occurred perhaps in the reign of Constantine III or later.' He argues that this was done to obtain silver without reducing the quantity of coins available. Some, perhaps most, of this silver was apparently used to make copies of siliquae (there were over 486 in the Hoxne hoard) that circulated together with official coins. The practice probably began after

[36] Ibid., 29.
[37] Ibid., 31–2.

402 when the supply of official siliquae ended, and may have continued after 409.[38] These forged and clipped siliquae suggest that some
Britons continued to use coins depicting the emperor two or three
decades after Constantine's departure.

The evidence of these coins is consistent with other indications,
notably the appeal to Aetius, the Roman general in Gaul, for help in
or soon after 446, that some British leaders continued, at least until
the middle of the century, to think that Britain was still part of the
Empire. No military reinforcements or imperial officials came to
Britain after 410, but contact with Gaul was maintained by church-
men. Germanus, bishop of Auxerre, with Lupus, bishop of Troyes,
visited Britain in 429 to combat heresy, and Germanus returned
c.435. Later in the century there are a few references to British bishops in Gaul. Some may have been exiles, but Gildas criticized bishops who sought consecration overseas, and in about 480 Constantius
of Lyon reported that the British Church was flourishing.[39] There
were also secular contacts across the Channel.[40] A remarkable
instance is the career of Riothamus, a British commander who,
shortly before 469, crossed to Gaul with a large force. Ian Wood has
suggested that he 'is perhaps best seen as a general who left Britain
because he wanted to serve the imperial cause, as indeed he did'.[41]

In the fifth and sixth centuries some Britons emigrated to north-
west Gaul where they created a new Britannia—Brittany. For a while
they continued to regard themselves as citizens of the Empire, and
their bishops participated in Gallic episcopal councils, but in the
sixth century Brittany became an 'alien enclave' in Gaul that was
then ruled by the Franks.[42] Another illustration of cross-Channel

---

[38] Ibid., 110–15. For other interpretations of clipping and coin imports in post-Roman
Britain, see Williams, 'Anglo-Saxon gold coinage'.

[39] Wood, 'The end of Roman Britain', 8–17, 22.

[40] Fifth-century trade between Britain and the Continent is discussed below.

[41] Wood, 'The fall of the Western Empire', 261.

[42] Charles-Edwards, *After Rome*, 6–8.

contact in the mid-fifth century is a hoard with fifty Roman coins, including sixteen solidi and four siliquae struck after 408, found at Patching in West Sussex in 1997. The coins were probably collected on the Continent and taken to Britain after 461.[43]

Although the central government of Britain must have broken down soon after the departure of Constantine III, the Roman system of civil government, with a council in each *civitas*, apparently continued for a while, but corporate government was unlikely to be effective for very long in the absence of Roman officials, backed by Roman arms. Internal conflicts and the need to counter invaders meant that power tended to pass into the hands of military leaders, some of whom were recognized as kings. Raids by Picts and Scots continued, but by the middle of the fifth century Germanic invaders from across the North Sea, called Saxons by both Gildas and Gallic chroniclers, were the main threat. They were well established in the south-east and by the end of the century had gained control of a kingdom in Kent.[44] Saxons were also active in Gaul in the fifth century, and some settled near Boulogne, Bayeux, in the lower Loire valley, and elsewhere. Archaeological evidence from early cemeteries suggests that some of these settlers may have reached Gaul via Britain, and there are tantalizing indications of later contacts between their descendants and Saxons in Britain.[45]

Early in the sixth century, Britons still ruled most of what had been Roman Britain, although according to Gildas, writing of his own time, 'external wars may have stopped, but not civil ones' (ch. 26). Anglo-Saxon immigration continued and by 600, with few exceptions, the only British, Christian kingdoms were in the west, while in a much larger area, from the Firth of Forth to the Channel in the south, a mixed population of Britons and Anglo-Saxon settlers were ruled by Anglo-Saxon kings.

---

[43] White, 'The Patching hoard'.
[44] Brooks, 'The creation and early structure of the kingdom of Kent'.
[45] Welch, 'Cross-Channel contacts'.

Very little is known about these English kingdoms until the end of the sixth century, but later evidence provides some clues to earlier developments. There is, for example, no doubt that there were many small kingdoms in the sixth century, as there were in the seventh, nor that some rulers succeeded in forcing others to submit and recognize them as overlords. Several seventh-century overlordships included most English kingdoms south of the Humber, and three Northumbrian kings also ruled British and Pictish kingdoms. Although none of these extensive empires survived their founders, submission to an overlord often led to permanent conquest; in fact all the eighth-century English kingdoms began as overlordships.[46]

Plunder was an important source of the wealth that kings needed to increase or maintain their authority. Gildas condemned kings for depending on plunder and adapted Isaiah to warn one of them that 'when you cease to plunder, then you will fall'.[47] Two centuries later Guthlac, a member of an Anglo-Saxon royal family, attempted to win power by taking up arms. He gathered companions and 'devastated the towns and residences of his foes, their villages and fortresses with fire and sword, and... amassed immense booty' before, aged 25, he turned to religion.[48] In the fifth and sixth centuries, slaves and livestock were the normal booty, for most of the treasure left by the Romans was concealed in hoards or, having been plundered by Picts and Scots, was in north Britain or Ireland.

In order to feed their households, retainers, and guests, kings normally stayed in royal estates where the food rents that their subjects were obliged to render were collected. As these, and other obligations, such as giving hospitality to kings and their agents, were customary throughout Britain and Ireland, it is likely that the Anglo-Saxon rulers took them over from their British predecessors.

[46] Sawyer, *From Roman Britain*, 48–9.
[47] *Gildas*, 32.5
[48] *Felix's Life of Saint Guthlac*, 80–3.

In all kingdoms except Kent, they also took over the system of land assessment used throughout the British Isles, based on the holdings of free men.[49] In Kent, the first Anglo-Saxon kingdom, assessments were in ploughlands (OE *sulung*), apparently a survival of the taxation system based on yokes (Latin *iuga*) that was used for all sorts of land throughout the Roman Empire in the fourth century.[50] Thanks to three centuries of Roman government, the rulers of lowland Britain in the fifth and sixth centuries apparently had greater rights than their contemporaries elsewhere in the British Isles.[51] Some prerogatives enjoyed by later English kings, for example the right to impose tolls and to control the production and distribution of salt, may have been acquired by Anglo-Saxons from British rulers.

Salt was needed to preserve meat, fish, butter, and cheese, and to make leather. It was extracted from sea-water at many places in the summer, but the brine springs at Droitwich and in Cheshire could be exploited all year and yielded far more and purer salt. In the seventeenth century, Droitwich brine contained three times as much salt as sea-water and therefore needed much less fuel to evaporate it, and the result was a dense, fine-grained salt that could be stored for a long time without liquefying.[52] Extensive excavations at Droitwich, the pre-Conquest charters of Worcester, and later texts, notably Domesday Book, show that salt was produced there continuously from pre-Roman times until the eighteenth century. In the fifth and sixth centuries only small amounts were produced, but by the eighth century, when Droitwich was controlled by Mercian kings, production had greatly increased and may have reached several hundred tons a year.[53]

---

[49] Charles-Edwards, 'Kinship, status and the origins of the hide'.

[50] Jones, *The Later Roman Empire*, 62–5.

[51] Sawyer, *From Roman Britain*, 73–4; Brooks, *Church, State and Access to Resources*.

[52] Maddicott, 'London and Droitwich', 25.

[53] Maddicott, 'London and Droitwich', 30–7. He concludes that 'Domesday production...may well have exceeded a thousand tons a year'.

The Cheshire brine-springs were also exploited by the Romans and probably by their successors. Although their salt was inferior to that produced at Droitwich, it was too valuable a resource to have been neglected by later rulers. In 1066 royal agents controlled the production of large quantities in Nantwich, Middlewich, and Northwich. These places were later the focus of an extensive network of 'saltways' reaching into Wales and across the Pennines that, like those radiating from Droitwich, were probably ancient.[54]

Although food-rents, tribute, and plunder were the main ways in which produce was distributed before the seventh century, there must have been some trade to exchange surplus produce. There are, indeed, indications that the later, well-attested, distribution pattern of Droitwich salt through major centres and along saltways and rivers was already established in the Iron Age.[55] Pottery may also have been distributed widely. It has been argued that tiny fragments of granite used to temper fifth- and sixth-century pottery found in many parts of east and midland England show that it was made in the Charnwood Forest area of Leicestershire.[56] This conclusion has been questioned, but one of the sceptics, John Hines, admits that the phenomenon 'urgently requires further research and explanation'.[57] In post-Roman Britain there may well have been markets held in connection with religious festivals or other traditional assemblies that, in the absence of new coins, have left no traces of the kind that enable metal-detectors to locate later 'productive sites' (these are discussed later in this chapter).

Texts and imported pottery show that in the fifth and sixth centuries there was trade between the western parts of the British Isles and the Roman Empire in which casks or barrels of wine, olive oil

---

[54] Thacker, 'Anglo-Saxon Cheshire', 241; Sawyer and Thacker, 'The Cheshire Domesday', 328–9, 365–6.

[55] Maddicott, 'London and Droitwich', 43–7; Blair, *Anglo-Saxon Oxfordshire*, 84–7.

[56] Williams and Vince, 'The characterization'.

[57] *Med. Arch.* 43 (1999), 311.

(probably in amphorae), and other goods were exchanged for slaves, leather goods, woollen cloth, and tin.[58] Some of this pottery found at several sites around the Irish Sea came from North Africa, but from about 475 to 550 most was from the heart of the Byzantine Empire, around the north-east Mediterranean, and was brought by ships with cargoes that were mainly assembled there, perhaps even in Constantinople.[59] Although some stopped en route at ports in the western Mediterranean, their destination was Britain. This traffic cannot have been on a large scale, but it was enough to yield other evidence of contacts between Byzantium and western Britain at that time, including sixth-century Byzantine coins, an inscription at Pen-machno in north Wales dated *in tempore iustini consiliis*, and the infor-mation about Britain reported by Procopius, some of whose informants had been in Britain.[60] After these direct contacts with the Mediterranean ended, the western parts of Britain, including Iona, continued to be supplied with wine and other goods from western Gaul.[61]

After 450 the situation was transformed by the growing power of the Franks ruled by Childeric, who for some time before his death (*c*.481) had been recognized as ruler of the Roman province of Belgica Secunda, which included Rheims and Boulogne. He was succeeded by his son Clovis who died in 511, having gained control of a large part of Gaul, including most of the north, and there are indications that he extended his authority across the Channel to Kent. For most of the sixth century his heirs claimed hegemony over part of south-ern Britain.[62] Frankish overlordship may explain the similarities between early Frankish and Kentish law, and the survival of the

[58] James, 'Ireland and western Gaul'; Thomas, 'Gallici Nautae'. For a detailed discus-sion of the contacts noted in this paragraph, see now, E. Campbell, *Continental and Medi-terranean Imports*.

[59] Fulford, 'Byzantium and Britain'.

[60] Griffiths, 'Markets and "productive sites"'; Thompson, 'Procopius'.

[61] James, 'Ireland and western Gaul', 375–8.

[62] Wood, *The Merovingian North Sea*, 10–18; James, *The Franks*, 103.

Roman system of land assessment in Kent but not in other parts of Britain.[63]

One result of Frankish control of the eastern Channel was that treasure was once again exported from Gaul to Britain and was soon used to furnish high-status graves in Kent. This treasure was drawn from the huge quantity that remained after the collapse of the western Empire, much of it held by aristocratic families and the churches they endowed, or by barbarian invaders. The stock of gold in western Europe was increased after 530 by the many coins that, until c.630, were sent to Germanic rulers by Byzantine emperors seeking support for their efforts to regain and retain control of Italy (see Figure 4). Many imperial coins circulated alongside copies made by the new rulers. By c.520 such quasi-imperial coins were produced by the Franks, who, unlike their contemporaries in Italy and Spain, did not treat coining as a royal monopoly; in sixth-century Gaul coins were struck for leading ecclesiastics, churches, towns, and magnates. Frankish kings produced some, but with the exception of Theodebert (533–548), they did not put their own names on gold coins until the 570s.[64]

In the sixth century treasure reached Kent in various ways; as gifts to generate or reward friendship, in marriage settlements, and some was probably brought by Frankish settlers. There is, however, little doubt that some, perhaps a great deal, was payment for slaves. The main trade route through Francia was then from Marseilles to the Rhineland, where slaves from Britain could be obtained for sale in Francia or Mediterranean markets such as Marseilles or Naples.[65] Links between Francia and south-east Britain began to be closer and are better documented in the time of Æthelberht, who succeeded his father as king of Kent c.590. His marriage some years earlier to Bertha,

---

[63] Above, p. 44; Wood, *The Merovingian North Sea*, 13.
[64] *MEC*, 92–3.
[65] McCormick, *Origins*, 625.

Figure 4. Solidus of Justinian I (527–565), issued 538–565, Constantinople mint. © Fitzwilliam Museum, Cambridge.

daughter of Charibert I, king of Paris (561–571), was not a prestigious match; Charibert dismissed her mother early in his reign, and was certainly dead when the marriage took place.[66] It did, however, prepare the way for the mission led by Augustine.[67] This opened new channels through which influences and treasure flowed from the Continent not only to Kent, but also to East Anglia and Northumbria

[66] Wood, *The Merovingian North Sea*, 15–16.
[67] Id., *The Merovingian Kingdoms*, 176–8.

and, by the end of the seventh century, to most parts of Anglo-Saxon England.[68]

The Anglo-Saxons did not produce their own coins until the seventh century, but by Æthelberht's reign (c.590–616) there was enough gold in Kent to enable his laws to specify penalties and compensations in *scillinga*, 'shillings', a word derived from a verb meaning 'to cut' (cf. ON *scilian*, modern Swedish *skilja*, 'to separate, cut off'). A shilling was a piece of gold weighing 20 Troy grains (1.3 g), the weight of a contemporary Frankish tremissis, cut from a ring or bar. In Æthelberht's laws the smaller unit of value was a gold fragment weighing a grain, i.e. a twentieth of a shilling, called a *sceat*, cognate with modern English 'shatter, scatter'.[69]

Many references in Bede's writings and other eighth-century texts show that in the seventh century treasure was distributed widely beyond Kent in many ways; to enrich churches, equip warriors, reward allies, pay tribute, or seize as plunder. In 2010 the abundance of gold after 650 was dramatically illustrated by the discovery in Staffordshire of a treasure hoard containing 5 kg of gold and 1.4 kg of silver broken into over 3400 fragments, many of them weighing less than 1.0 g. Most of the identifiable objects were war-gear (sword hilts, some with garnet inlay, and at least one helmet), but there were at least two crosses and a strip with an inscription from the Old Testament.[70]

In the sixth century, when most cross-Channel traffic passed through Kent, many crossings must have been made by small craft that travelled between landing places, some of which may have been used before the Roman conquest.[71] Large vessels and those carrying high-status passengers probably used the main fourth-century

[68] Campbell, 'The first century'; Wood, 'The Franks and Sutton Hoo'; Fletcher, 'The influence of Merovingian Gaul'.

[69] *MEC*, 15.

[70] Leahy and Bland, *The Staffordshire Hoard*; Med. Arch. 54 (2010), 390–1.

[71] McGrail, 'Boats and boatmanship'.

Roman ports: Dover, Richborough, Reculver, and, across the Channel, Boulogne which had been controlled by the Franks since the reign of Childeric.[72] The increased traffic in the seventh century and its spread beyond Kent is reflected by the revival of ports in London and York, and the creation of new ones at Ipswich and *Hamwic*, discussed in the next chapter. On the Continent, exports from the Paris region, in particular wine, were shipped through Rouen, but archaeological evidence and coins, together with reports of cross-Channel journeys, show that Quentovic replaced Boulogne and that routes through the huge delta formed by the rivers Scheldt, Meuse, and Rhine increased with the revival of Domburg/Walcheren and the rapid development of a new port at Dorestad.[73]

There are many indications that cross-Channel traffic in gifts and traded goods increased after 600. Slaves, many of them war-booty, are the only English export for which there is evidence in contemporary texts. The first is a letter that Pope Gregory sent in 595 to his priest Candidus ordering him to use income from papal estates in Gaul to buy English boys (*pueri Angli*) aged 17 or 18, probably in Marseilles, to be trained in God's service.[74] The slave trade continued through the seventh century.[75] It is, however, likely that wealthy Franks and the monasteries they founded also wanted other English produce, for example lead, clothing, hunting dogs, and even food, which is known to have been exported to Francia later (see Chapter 4). In return the Anglo-Saxons obtained wine and other Frankish produce as well as treasure. The wine fair of St Denis, founded by Dagobert in 634, was already attracting Anglo-Saxon merchants in the reign of his son Clovis II (639–657).[76] Other imports that have been

[72] Milne, 'Maritime traffic'; Wood, *The Merovingian Kingdoms*, 40–1.
[73] Wood, *The Merovingian Kingdoms*, 293–5; *MEC*, 134–7; Coupland, 'Trading places'. See now, Lebecq et al., *Quentovic*.
[74] *EHD*, no. 161.
[75] Pelteret, 'Slave raiding'.
[76] Levison, *England and the Continent*, 7–8; Pertz, *Diplomata*, no. 77, trans. Murray, *From Roman to Merovingian Gaul*, 585–9.

found in seventh-century contexts in several parts of Anglo-Saxon England, such as purple amethyst beads, 'cabochon' garnets, cowrie shells, and elephant ivory, had presumably reached Francia via Marseille.[77] Recent studies of Marseilles based on archaeological and numismatic as well as written evidence have shown that very large quantities of produce from around the Mediterranean and beyond were imported into Francia in the sixth and early seventh centuries, and distributed widely, even as far as Frisia.[78]

Tolls on these imports were a valuable source of revenue for Frankish kings, who also exacted tolls on goods transported by road or river through Francia. The surviving privileges granting some major monasteries exemption from tolls are good evidence for this traffic. The most detailed list is a diploma of Chilperic II dated 716, confirming privileges granted over 50 years earlier to Corbie Abbey in north Francia.[79] It is unreliable as evidence for the early eighth century, but is more trustworthy for the mid-seventh century when the original grant was made. The specific exemptions from tolls on imports include 30 lb of pepper, 150 lb of cumin, 2 lb of cloves, 1 lb of cinnamon, 50 lb of dates, 100 lb of figs, 30 lb of pistachios, 20 lb of rice, 10 goat skins from Cordova, and 50 quires of papyrus.

There is no reason to doubt that some of the exotic goods imported through Marseilles, together with Frankish produce such as wine and olive oil, were already reaching England before 600, as they certainly did in the seventh century. The main recipients were initially rulers and magnates, who were best able to supply the slaves and other exports that were in demand in Francia, but in the seventh century churches and clergy in England needed wine, oil, fine vestments, church furnishings, books, and many other imports. In the second half of the century, religious communities dramatically increased

---

[77] Hinton, *Gold and Gilt*, 68.
[78] Loseby, 'Marseille and the Pirenne Thesis'.
[79] Pertz, *Diplomata* no. 86; Loseby, 'Marseille and the Pirenne Thesis II', 178–89.

the demand for such imports. By 700 kings, bishops, magnates, and their relatives had founded at least seventy such communities, many of them with large endowments, ranging from 40 to 100 hides.[80] Apart from meeting their own needs, many soon became local, even regional, economic centres, with markets in which they could sell imported goods as well as surplus produce from their own estates and workshops, and which also provided opportunities for local farmers and craftsmen to trade.[81]

Gold coins, mostly Merovingian tremisses, continued to be imported into England for most of the seventh century. Sixty-two have been found in two hoards; thirty-seven in the ship-burial at Sutton Hoo that has been dated c.625, and twenty-five in a hoard deposited at Crondall c.650. (A possible, but very badly recorded, hoard was found in 1848 in the river at Kingston-on-Thames.) In 1975 Stuart Rigold published a list of over 100 others that were found separately, over half of them from graves in which they were used as jewellery or offerings.[82] In the next 30 years, over forty other imported gold coins of the sixth and seventh centuries were found, mostly by metal detector users.[83]

The earliest English gold coin is a tremissis of Frankish type struck in Canterbury soon after Augustine began his mission in Kent. It was, however, not until the 630s that an English coinage of gold shillings or thrymsas began to be produced in mints in Kent, London, and perhaps elsewhere in the south-east (see Figure 5). The Crondall hoard, which contained sixty-nine English coins,[84] supplemented by a few single finds, shows that by about 650 this English coinage was on a very small scale. All but nine of the Crondall coins are die-linked

---

[80] Blair, *The Church*, 87; Wood, 'La richesse'.

[81] This happened earlier in Francia; Lebecq, 'The role of monasteries in the systems of production'.

[82] Rigold, 'The Sutton Hoo coins'.

[83] Abdy and Williams, 'A catalogue'.

[84] Seventy-three according to Metcalf, *Thrymsas and Sceattas*, 2.

with others in the hoard, and eleven of the fourteen contemporary coins found elsewhere before c.1985 are also die-linked with coins from Crondall. This evidence led Grierson to conclude that 'the coinage before c.650 was indeed very small and used by a limited group of people for special purposes or transactions...in marked contrast to the later gold coinage where the finds are more plentiful and there are few die-links between them'.[85] Ian Stewart, who accepted this judgement, has argued that in the seventh century 'the boundary between coin, jewellery and bullion was vague and variable'.[86] Gold coins could have been treated simply as bullion, but the existence of seventh-century forgeries suggests that they were then being treated as currency.

In the late seventh century the gold coinage in England and most of Francia was replaced by one exclusively of silver.[87] This change, which happened in the 670s, has sometimes been explained by the decline in the amount of gold in western Europe, reflected in the gradual debasement of gold in the seventh century, resulting in what is known as 'pale gold'. This was mainly due to the ending of Byzantine gold subsidies to western rulers early in the 630s.[88] Philip Grierson has, however, convincingly argued that the change was rather a response to the needs of the developing market economy for more convenient coins of lower value than the earlier gold ones.[89] This need was partly met in England after about 650 by the increased production of more heavily debased, and therefore less valuable, thrymsas.

The change to a completely silver coinage began in Neustria shortly before 670 and soon afterwards in England.[90] Within little more than a decade, the coinage in south-east England, most of

[85] MEC, 160–1.
[86] Stewart, 'The English and Norman mints', 11.
[87] MEC, 93–5, 163–4.
[88] Grierson, *Coins of Medieval Europe*, 19–20.
[89] Ibid., 20; MEC, 95–6.
[90] This and the next two paragraphs are based on MEC, 93–5, 149–59.

Figure 5. a. Merovingian gold tremissis, Charibert II (629–632), Banassic mint. b. Anglo-Saxon pale gold thrymsa, Two Emperors type, *c.*630–640. © Fitzwilliam Museum, Cambridge.

Francia, the lower Rhineland, and Frisia consisted exclusively of silver pennies (in contemporary Old English texts *pening; denarius* in Francia). Initially they had the same weight and diameter as their gold predecessors. Some had designs based on earlier coins, but many completely new designs were also used. Thanks to a misunderstanding, since the seventeenth century these English and Frisian pennies have often been called 'sceattas', and that name will be used here to distinguish them from the broader-flan pennies that replaced them in the mid-eighth century.

Die-links provide valuable clues to the changing volume of English coinage in the seventh century, but the interpretation of the role of gold coins in seventh-century England is hampered by the impossibility of estimating how many imported coins were circulating. Gold was worth at least ten times as much as silver and great care was taken not to lose gold coins or other gold objects, or to recover any that were lost. The archaeological elusiveness of gold is well

illustrated by the fact that although large numbers of 'bezants'—
Byzantine gold coins—were used in England in the twelfth and thirteenth centuries, none has been found.[91] The number of single gold
coins that have been found is, therefore, likely to give a misleading
impression of the number that were in circulation. Comparison
between the numbers of gold and silver coins found on a site must
take account of this.[92] It is therefore significant that some sixth- or
seventh-century gold coins have been found in places where, as
argued later in this chapter, concentrations of silver sceattas of the
late seventh and early eighth centuries, together with contemporary
artefacts, reveal the existence of markets, some of which continued
for centuries. Tremisses and solidi found on such sites suggest that
they were already trading places in the first half of the seventh century, and perhaps earlier. Rigold himself drew attention to the evidence from Reculver, a Roman fort at the north end of the Wantsum
Channel, an important tidal waterway between the Thames and the
Channel, where a monastery was founded c.670. Finds from the
eroded site made in the seventeenth and eighteenth centuries include
well over sixty-five sceattas and four earlier Frankish tremisses,
showing that it 'was clearly a major port throughout the seventh and
early eighth centuries'.[93] More remarkably, the site of a Roman farm
at Coddenham, near Ipswich, has yielded 250 mid-Saxon artefacts
and sixty-five coins dated c.600–720, including three Merovingian
tremisses, a cut quarter and two forgeries, twelve English thrymsas,
and fifty sceattas.[94] Mark Blackburn has noted seven other similar
sites in east England, from Kent to Lincolnshire, which have yielded
early gold coins.[95] These could have been treated simply as weights

[91] Cook, 'The bezant in Angevin England'; Blackburn, 'Gold in England'.
[92] Metcalf, 'The availability and uses of gold coinage'; id., 'Merovingian and Frisian
gold'.
[93] Rigold, 'The Sutton Hoo coins', 662.
[94] Newman, 'Exceptional finds', 103–6.
[95] Blackburn, '"Productive" sites', 32.

of the metal, but the discovery of forgeries and, at Coddenham, a cut quarter suggests that they were already being used as currency in the first half of the seventh century. Another remarkable concentration of early coin finds, formerly located vaguely in 'South Lincolnshire', is now known to be near Spalding, on the Welland. So far some 200 coins have been discovered there, mostly sceattas with at least a dozen Merovingian tremisses, three of them sixth-century. This was apparently an important centre for trade with Francia that by-passed Kent.[96]

A few sceattas have inscriptions, most apparently representing the names of moneyers, who seem to have had a great deal of autonomy. The fact that rulers are named on coins only in Northumbria makes it doubtful whether the English sceattas produced south of the Humber were royal issues. The weight and fineness of the early sceattas seem to have been carefully regulated throughout the area in which they were made. This is more likely to have been due to the influence of merchants than to agreement between rulers on both sides of the Channel. The sceattas have, indeed, been described as the coinage of a trading nexus,[97] an interpretation supported by the copying or adaptation of some designs in widely separated areas; for example, some designs originating in Frisia or the lower Rhineland were later used in England (see Figure 6).

By the end of the century, remarkably large quantities of sceattas were being produced in Frisia and the lower Rhineland by moneyers who had suddenly acquired an unprecedented quantity of silver. The source is not known; it was probably in Germany.[98] They were consequently able for a while to produce a huge quantity of sceattas, which were dispersed widely in western Francia and up the Rhine,

---

[96] Metcalf, 'Mercian and Frisian gold'.

[97] Wood, *The Merovingian Kingdoms*, 301.

[98] Spufford, *Money and its Use*, 32, tentatively suggested that this Frisian silver came from Francia. This is unlikely; very few Merovingian deniers have been found in England; Metcalf, 'Betwixt sceattas', 18–20, 30–1.

a   b

Figure 6. a. Frisian sceat, Series E/'Porcupine' type, *c.*695–760. b. Anglo-Saxon sceat, Æthelred type, *c.*695–720. © Fitzwilliam Museum, Cambridge.

and very large numbers reached England. They 'circulated more widely than the Anglo-Saxon issues had done and quickly came to dominate the currency, constituting for example two-thirds of the 324 coins from the Aston Rowant, Oxfordshire, hoard, deposited *c.*710'.[99] Well over half the sceattas recorded as single finds in Lincolnshire by 1994 were from Frisia and the Lower Rhineland.[100]

Many of these imported sceattas were melted down and the silver was used to strike English sceattas.[101] As a result, in the early eighth century there was a dramatic increase in the number of coins circulating in eastern and southern England. This is clearly demonstrated by the number of coins that were lost accidentally and have been discovered as single finds by chance, by archaeologists, and, since the 1970s, by metal detector users. By 2000 some 6500 coins struck between 600 and 1180 had been discovered and recorded. The rate of

[99] Blackburn, 'Money and coinage', 546.
[100] Sawyer, *Anglo-Saxon Lincolnshire*, 253–61.
[101] The rest of this chapter is based on Blackburn, '"Productive" sites'.

loss depends partly on how frequently coins changed hands, but the main factor was the number of coins in circulation. The fact that almost all the coins circulating in England between the late seventh and twelfth centuries can be dated within two or three decades has enabled Mark Blackburn to estimate the rate at which coins were lost in successive 25-year periods in various places and regions. Figure 7 shows the overall pattern, based on 3,552 coins found singly in England south of the Humber before 2003. In general the chronological pattern of coin loss, and therefore of the number of coins in circulation, was much the same in most parts of eastern England. The surprising, even startling, implication is that there were more coins circulating in eastern England, many of them from Frisia and the lower Rhineland, in the first years of the eighth century than at any time before the Norman Conquest.

This flood of silver into England from the Rhineland and Frisia shows that the English were then producing a substantial surplus of goods for which there was a lively demand across the Channel. In return, a variety of continental produce, especially pottery, was imported to England. The fact that very few Frankish deniers have

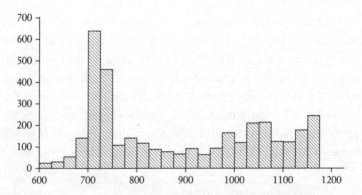

Figure 7. Histogram: Single finds of coins minted 600–1180, found in southern England by 2000. (From Blackburn, '"Productive" sites', fig. 3.2, p. 32.)

been found in England suggests that the trade with western Francia was evenly balanced, but that trade with markets east of the Rhine yielded a great deal of silver, as it did in the late tenth and eleventh centuries. Much of this trade passed through major emporia that, with the exception of *Hamwic* (Southampton), founded *c.*700, were all in the east, from York to London and Kent. Their role in the English economy is discussed in the next chapter. It is, however, first necessary to take account of the numismatic and archaeological evidence that reveals the existence of many other markets that are not mentioned in contemporary texts.

In numerous places, most of them in eastern England, large numbers of sceattas together with buckles, strap ends, brooches, pins, and other artefacts have been found in quite small areas. Some of these places may have been where rulers or other wealthy people lived, and some may have been sites of unrecorded religious communities, but when the sequence of coins begins in the early eighth century and continues to the twelfth or even later, it seems more likely that they were places in which people gathered and traded.[102] A good example is a site near West Ravendale, west of Grimsby, where eight early eighth-century sceattas have been found together with coins of Edgar, Æthelred II, and Stephen. From the middle of the eighth century to the end of the tenth, when there were far fewer coins in circulation, the site has yielded a ninth-century Northumbrian coin and a quantity of ninth-century metal artefacts. There are also later medieval finds, the most remarkable being two tumbrels for weighing fourteenth-century coins.

Mark Blackburn has discussed over thirty sites where concentrations of sceattas have been found. Four were emporia (*Hamwic*, Ipswich, London, York), three were monasteries (Reculver, Whitby,

---

[102] Hutcheson, 'The origins', 80–2, has argued that some 'productive sites' in East Anglia were estate or administrative centres in which food-rents were collected. If so, the coins and other objects found were presumably lost in markets where some of the produce was sold.

Whithorn), one was a high-status settlement at Flixborough in Lincolnshire that may have housed a religious community in the eighth century,[103] and twenty-seven are similar to the one near West Ravensdale described above. These confirm that there was a significant increase in marketing at the end of the seventh century. The fact that earlier gold coins have been found at nine of them suggests that the commercial expansion began before the church had much influence. Most of these sites are in eastern England, many of them in areas that were later important for sheep rearing, close to the coast or rivers that gave access to other parts of England and to the Continent. It is, therefore, likely that the most valuable exports were no longer slaves but, as later, wool, cloth, and clothing. The evidence for these rural markets or fairs also casts doubt on the claim that the major emporia monopolized the import of prestige goods, a topic discussed in the next chapter.

[103] Loveluck, 'A high-status Anglo-Saxon settlement at Flixborough'.

4

The Eighth and Ninth Centuries

Contemporary texts show that after about 650 there was a great deal of traffic across the Channel. Most reported voyages were made by clergy on church business; missionaries, messengers carrying letters and gifts, and pilgrims travelling to Rome. Some people are known to have crossed the Channel several times; between 652 and 703 Benedict Biscop and Wilfrid each made five return journeys, and in 716 Ceolfrith died in Francia on his fifth journey south. The traffic between England and the Continent continued on a substantial scale at least until the early ninth century and made possible the extensive contacts revealed by the correspondence of Boniface, Lull, Alcuin, and Lupus of Ferrières, as well as the rapid spread of news between England and the Continent.[1]

A few accounts of voyages say where they began and ended, naming harbours or, more often, regions. For example, in 678 Wilfrid sailed to Frisia, and in 716 Boniface travelled from London to Dorestad.[2] Rouen was another destination, but the most frequently named continental harbour was Quentovic, described by Stephanus as 'on

---

[1] Story, *Carolingian Connections*, 93–133, 224–43.
[2] Stephanus, *Vita Wilfridi*, ch. 26; Willibald, *Vita Bonifatii*, ch. 4.

the most direct route (*via rectissima*) to the Holy See'.[3] Most of the frequently named English destinations were in the south-east. In 652 Wilfrid's first journey to Rome, with Benedict Biscop, began in Kent, and in 703 he landed there on his way to London after his last visit to Italy.[4] It was from London that Boniface sailed to Dorestad in 716 and to Quentovic 2 years later.[5] The normal route from London to Quentovic was by the Wantsum, a tidal channel 'about three furlongs (c.600 m) wide' separating Thanet from the rest of Kent, which also gave access to Fordwich, the port of Canterbury.[6] A charter dated 763/4 shows that there was a toll station at Sarre on its north shore.[7] A century earlier, when Wilfrid returned from his consecration in Gaul, he arrived at the port of Sandwich (*in portum Sandwicae*), which lay at the southern entrance to the Wantsum channel; he probably continued his journey through it.[8] There are very few references to harbours or landing places in other parts of England. In 720 Willibald and his brother sailed to the Seine from Hamblemouth, about 8 km from *Hamwic*.[9] Alcuin's description of York as a centre of commerce, comparable with London, is confirmed by the report in the *Life of Liudger* that Frisian merchants fled from the city in 773.[10] Ian Wood has recently drawn attention to the fact that Jarrow stood on the shore of one of the great natural harbours of the north of England, Jarrow Slake.[11]

The contrast between the numerous references to Kent as a destination and the very few about journeys to or from other parts of England gives a misleading impression of the traffic between England

---

[3] Stephanus, *Vita Wilfridi*, ch. 25.

[4] Ibid., chs. 33, 57.

[5] *HE* ii. 3; Willibald, *Vita Bonifatii*, ch. 5.

[6] *HE* i. 25.

[7] S 29.

[8] Stephanus, *Vita Wilfridi*, ch. 13.

[9] Hygeburg, *Vita Willibaldi*, ch. 3.

[10] Rollason, *Sources*, 129–32; for the date, Story, *Carolingian Connections*, 146.

[11] Wood, 'The origins of Jarrow'; id., 'Monasteries and the geography of power'.

and the Continent. Alcuin's letters and the exceptionally detailed information about Francia in Northumbrian annals show that there were very close contacts between Northumbria and Francia in the eighth century. This suggests that a significant number of ships from the Continent arriving in Kent continued further north to the Humber or beyond. Some voyages from ports in eastern and northern England may have bypassed Kent, but many did not. For example, early in 808 the exiled Northumbrian king Eardwulf travelled to Nijmegen to appeal for help from Charlemagne. There is reason to believe that en route he was given refuge by Wulfred, archbishop of Canterbury.[12] The anonymous *Life of Ceolfrith* includes an account of his last journey in 716 with tantalizing information about his voyage to Francia.[13] He travelled overland, staying briefly at *Cornu vallis*, identified by Richard Morris as Kirkdale, before boarding a ship on 4 July at the mouth of the Humber.[14] Before he reached Gaul on 12 August his ship 'was brought to land in three provinces, in each of which he was honourably received by all and held in veneration'. These provinces presumably included East Anglia and Kent.

The ship on which Ceolfrith sailed, with about eighty companions, had been carefully prepared in Wearmouth or Jarrow.[15] Kings and people of high status probably travelled, like Ceolfrith, in their own ships, but most people going to the Continent must have done so on ships that were making the journey anyway, carrying traders and goods. In 716 Boniface paid his fare to the captain of a ship that was returning to Dorestad from London, and 4 years later Willibald similarly paid for his passage from Hamblemouth to Rouen.[16] Some traders who owned ships acted as agents for monasteries or other major landowners. A good example is Ibbo, a Frisian merchant who gave

[12] Story, *Carolingian Connections*, 202.
[13] *Vita Ceolfridi*, chs. 31–2.
[14] Morris, *Journeys from Jarrow*, 19–23.
[15] *Vita Ceolfridi*, ch. 22.
[16] Hygeburg, *Life of Willibald*, ch. 3; Willibald, *Vita Bonifatii*, ch. 4.

himself to the community of St Maximin in Trier with all his fortune, including his ship, and continued to make journeys across the sea to buy goods for the monastery. On one occasion he was accompanied by six other merchant ships that were not serving that community.[17]

In the early eighth century some English religious communities also had their own ships to export their produce and import goods, on which royal tolls were normally levied. Twelve royal charters dated between 733 and 764 granted exemption from toll at London, Fordwich, and Sarre to ships belonging to the bishops and cathedral communities of London, Rochester, and Worcester (two ships), and to the monasteries of Reculver and Minster in Thanet (three ships).[18] One of these privileges, probably issued in 763–764, by King Eadbald II of Kent to Minster in Thanet, reserving the king's right to pre-empt any merchandise brought to Fordwich, has been described as 'welcome and explicit evidence that the vessels to which toll-privileges applied were actually engaged in some kind of commercial activity'.[19] It is likely that many other wealthy religious communities also had their own ships, some of which were granted similar toll exemptions that have not survived.

English exports are rarely specified. The few early references to the sale of slaves overseas and to English slaves on the Continent have been interpreted as cumulative evidence that the slave trade was on a fairly large scale.[20] Most other exports mentioned in contemporary texts were gifts. In 758 Cuthbert, abbot of Wearmouth and Jarrow, sent Lul knives, a robe of otterskin, and 'two palls of subtle workmanship, one white, one coloured'.[21] In 852 Lupus of Ferrières asked Æthelwulf, king of Wessex, for lead to roof his church, and 30 years

[17] Lebecq, 'Long distance merchants'; McCormick, *Origins*, 656, who suggests, 129–31 n. 2, that Willibald travelled in a convoy.
[18] Kelly, 'Trading privileges'.
[19] S 29; Kelly, *Charters of St Augustine's*, 182.
[20] Pelteret, 'Slave raiding and trading', 104–5; cf. McCormick, *Origins*, 738–9.
[21] Tangl, *Die Briefe*, no. 116 (*EHD* no. 185).

later Fulk, archbishop of Rheims, thanked King Alfred for the gift of dogs 'of noble stock and excellent'.[22] Apart from manuscripts, the gifts from England most frequently mentioned in eighth-century letters were garments. Æthelberht, king of Kent, sent Boniface two woollen cloaks, and in 773 Alhred, king of Northumbria, and his wife Osgifu sent twelve cloaks to Lull.[23] It is, therefore, likely that textiles were an important commercial export. This is confirmed by Charlemagne's complaint in 796 about the size of cloaks sent from Mercia.[24] The complaint was echoed by Notker the Stammerer's report that Charlemagne protested vigorously that the Frisians were selling short cloaks at the same price as large ones, which suggests that Frisians were selling cloaks made in England.[25] Elsewhere Notker describes Frisian cloaks as expensive and variously coloured white, grey, crimson, and sapphire.[26] The importance of England as a source of clothing is underlined by Lupus of Ferrières' protest that because his abbey had lost the cell of St-Josse, near Quentovic, his monks did not receive their accustomed clothing and were forced to wear 'garments worn and darned in many places'.[27] He also blamed the loss of St-Josse for the reduced supply of vegetables, fish, cheese, wax, and corn.[28] It is surprising that Ferrières was so dependent on Quentovic, 280 km distant, for a supply of such things; they may have been English exports, but they could have been brought to Quentovic by coastal traffic.

There is no direct textual evidence for any commercial imports to England in the eighth and ninth centuries, but some things sent as

[22] Loup de Ferrières, *Correspondance*, no. 84; Birch, *Cartularium Saxonicum*, no. 555 (for 556) (*EHD* no. 223).

[23] Tangl, *Die Briefe*, nos. 105 (Emerton, no. 85) and 121 (*EHD* no. 187).

[24] Alcuin, *Epistolae*, no. 100 (*EHD* no. 197). Hinton, *Gold and Gilt*, 89–90, suggests that this 'royal discourse was about gift exchange', but Nelson, 'Carolingian contacts', 142, points out that the gifts mentioned in this letter 'go in just one direction, from Charlemagne to select Anglo-Saxons'.

[25] Notker, *Gesta Karoli*, i. 34 (trans. Thorpe, 47–8).

[26] Id., *Gesta Karoli*, ii. 9 (trans. Thorpe, 63).

[27] Loup de Ferrières, *Correspondance*, no. 42.

[28] Ibid., nos. 43, 45, 47. Cf. Nelson, 'England and the Continent', 17–19.

gifts, such as spices, wine, and goat-hair textiles, were presumably also traded.[29] A letter written by Alcuin in 790, when he was in Northumbria, to Joseph, one his pupils in Francia, is particularly revealing. He asked Joseph to send 'three-ply garments of goat-hair and wool for the use of the boys, both lay and clerical, and linen for my own use and black and red goat-hair hoods, if you can find any, and plenty of paints of fine sulphur (presumably to illuminate manuscripts) and dyes for colouring'. In the same letter he complains about a lack of wine and asks Joseph to help send 'two cart loads of the best clear wine' that had been promised.[30] In another letter written in 790 he complained that 'oil is now almost unobtainable in Britain'.[31] There is an interesting reference to wine in a list of the annual food rent owed by an estate in Kent in the early ninth century to Christ Church, Canterbury, including 'a measure of honey and twice as much wine, whichever they can get at the time'.[32]

There is good evidence for cross-Channel trade in the reign of Charlemagne who, in a dispute with Offa in 790, threatened to prohibit traders from Britain landing in Gaul.[33] According to Alcuin, the result was that English and Frankish traders were forbidden to sail.[34] Six years later Charlemagne protested that some English merchants claimed to be pilgrims and therefore exempt from toll, and demanded that the 'ancient law of trading', giving foreign merchants the right to appeal to royal justice, should protect Frankish merchants in Offa's kingdom, as English merchants were protected in Charlemagne's.[35]

[29] Tangl, *Die Briefe*, nos. 49, 74–6, 91 (Emerton nos. 39, 58–60, 74); Alcuin, *Epistolae*, no. 226 (Allott no. 19).

[30] Alcuin, *Epistolae*, no. 8 (Allott no. 9).

[31] Ibid., no. 7 (Allott no. 31).

[32] S 1188.

[33] *EHD* no. 20.

[34] Alcuin, *Epistolae*, no. 7 (Allott no. 31; *EHD* no. 192).

[35] Ibid., no. 100 (Allott no. 40; *EHD* no. 197). Cf. Alcuin's letter to Remigius, bishop of Chur, commending a merchant to his protection and help in avoiding delays by toll-collectors, *Epistolae*, no. 77 (Allott no. 158).

The few earlier references to cross-Channel commerce give a misleading impression of its scale. A better guide is the flow of Frisian coins into England and their wide dispersal in the early eighth century, discussed in Chapter 3. The fact that several coastal trading places, many of them called *wic*, flourished throughout that century clearly shows that overseas trade continued despite the substantial reductions in the number and weight of Frisian coins imported after *c*.720.

By *c*.750 three of the main *wics* so far identified, *Lundenwic*, *Hamwic*, and Ipswich (the only one not mentioned in contemporary texts), had all expanded to their full size (50–65 ha). They were apparently populous communities with regular street plans in which many crafts were practised, and were centres for regional and overseas trade.[36] Another, *Eoforwic*, which appears to have begun *c*.700, has been found close to York. The excavated area (1200 m^2) was abandoned *c*.750 and was later covered with domestic rubbish before it was reoccupied about 50 years later, but with no sign of foreign trade or contacts. There are, however, indications that, as might be expected, the *wic* was larger.[37] The fact that no trace has been found of the Frisian merchants who left York in 773 suggests that they, and perhaps others, operated elsewhere along the bank of the River Foss.

Imports found in all these *wics*, including Frisian coins, unfinished lava mill-stones from Mayen in the Rhineland, and pottery from a wide arc south of the Channel from the Loire and Normandy to the Rhineland and Low Countries, show that in the eighth and early ninth centuries their contacts were as extensive, if not so intensive, as those of London in the eleventh (discussed in Chapter 5). Very few traces of perishable imports such as spices, wine, and olive oil have

---

[36] Hill and Cowie, *Wics*; Astill, 'General survey', 32–4; Hinton, 'The large towns', 218–21; Moreland, 'The significance of production', 72–8.

[37] Hill and Cowie, *Wics*, 92–4; Kemp, *Anglian Settlement at 46–54 Fishergate*; O'Connor, *Bones from 46–54 Fishergate*.

so far been detected, but a barrel used to line a well in Ipswich was made with wood from a tree felled in the Rhineland soon after 873, and was presumably used to ship wine.[38]

Little of the imported pottery was distributed, probably because there was little demand for it.[39] Coins and mill-stones were, however, widely distributed,[40] although not all were imported through these four major *wics*; reasons are given below for thinking that there were many other landing places through which goods were imported. Although most of the pottery found in these *wics* was made locally, a little came from other parts of England, showing that they all had extensive contacts inland. At *Hamwic*, for example, 80 per cent of the pottery was made locally, but small quantities may have come from Surrey, or from the Charnwood Forest in Leicestershire, while Maxey type ware from Cambridgeshire reached York.[41] An improved type of pottery began to be made in Ipswich *c.*720 and by the middle of the century was distributed widely in eastern England from York to Kent, and in the Midlands as far as Oxford; a little reached *Hamwic*. The main concentration outside East Anglia was in *Lundenwic* where, on the Royal Opera House site, in the first half of the ninth century 60 per cent of the sherds (81 per cent by weight) were Ipswich ware; as Lyn Blackmore points out, this distribution must reflect trade rather than reciprocal exchanges.[42] With the exception of Ipswich ware, the produce of the major *wics* was not distinctive; it is therefore not possible to determine how far it was distributed. The metal and bone objects made in the *wics* were very similar to those made in many other places.[43] Rough cloth was made in most communities, perhaps

---

[38] Wade, 'Ipswich', 255.

[39] Brown, 'The social significance'; Morton, 'Distribution', 123–8.

[40] Blackburn, 'Productive sites'; Palmer, 'The Hinterlands'; Parkhouse, 'The distribution'.

[41] Blackmore, 'Pottery: trade and tradition', 25–7, 34.

[42] Ibid., 27, 36.

[43] Hinton, *Gold and Gilt*, 92–7.

in most households, but there is no evidence that better-quality fabrics were made in the major *wics*.

Although only a small part of the major *wics* (less than 5 per cent) has been excavated, the discovered remains suggest that large areas within them were densely occupied. *Hamwic* has yielded whole or partial plans of 130 buildings, 1450 rubbish pits and wells, and eight small cemeteries, and in *Lundenwic* sixty-three buildings (some of them superimposed) have been found on the site of the Royal Opera House.[44] Cemeteries associated with continental *wics* provide some basis for estimating their populations, but as few eighth- and ninth-century graves have been found in or near the major English *wics*, it is only possible to guess how many people lived in them; the guess for *Hamwic* is 3000.[45]

Large quantities of animal bones found in the major *wics* were mainly of cattle, with some sheep and pigs. This limited variety has been interpreted as evidence that the *wics* were part of a tributary economy and that their food was not bought, but supplied from food-rents of kings and, perhaps, others.[46] Food-rents could, however, have supplied a great deal of other produce and were, moreover, an improbable source for the relatively large number of sheep that were several years old and had, presumably, been kept for their wool, or for the numerous and varied fish remains found in *Lundenwic*.[47] It is more likely that they were supplied from nearby farms and through markets like those at Canterbury, but that their inhabitants, unlike those of Canterbury, could not afford luxuries and had to be content with much the same diet as most of the English, in which the basic ingredients were bread and gruel made from cereals. In *Lundenwic* almost every household had a hand quern.[48] In the early ninth

---

[44] Hill and Cowie, *Wics*, 87–92.
[45] Ibid., 67–74
[46] Ibid., 7–13, 54–60.
[47] Cowie, 'Mercian London', 205.
[48] Ibid., 204.

century Archbishop Wulfred provided for the distribution of bread with cheese or lard to 2000 paupers in Canterbury on the anniversary of his death, and a century later Athelstan ordered that destitute men should be regularly given bread and bacon or mutton.[49]

The major *wics* did not monopolize overseas trade. Many other harbours or landing places on or accessible to the coast were used in the eighth century. Most appear to have been associated with minsters. For example, in Kent Fordwich was the harbour for Christ Church and St Augustines in Canterbury, Minster in Thanet and Reculver were certainly trading across the Channel as, probably, Folkestone, Dover, and Minster in Sheppey were, as well as Tilbury and Barking on the Thames. *Sandtun*, west of Hythe, was a small seasonal fishing settlement that was a centre for coastal and cross-Channel trade from the seventh century to the end of the ninth.[50] A third of the pottery found there was imported from northern Francia, and the seventeen coins, most found by metal detector users, included a seventh-century tremissis from Quentovic, a mid-eighth-century denier from Dorestad, and several sceattas including one struck in Frisia in the early eighth century. In 732 land there was granted to the nearby minster at Lyminge for salt making.[51] Presumably *Sandtun* also supplied it with fish and imports from the Continent.[52]

Archaeological evidence suggests that numerous minsters on or near the east coast were also trading overseas. James Campbell has emphasized the importance of sea traffic and trade in Cuthbert's Northumbria, and has drawn attention to Professor Hill's observation that a striking number of monasteries lay beside harbours. He has himself suggested that the meeting at Whitby in 664 'is much

---

[49] S 1414; Athelstan's Charity Ordinance, Attenborough, *Laws*, 126–7.
[50] Gardiner et al., 'Continental trade and non-urban ports'.
[51] S 23. S 270 is a ninth- or tenth-century forgery that was apparently intended to confirm that the minster possessed considerably more land there.
[52] Kelly, 'Lyminge Minster'.

more likely to have been arranged there for the convenience of those who travelled by water than that of those who travelled by land'.[53] Most, probably all, inland minsters were similarly associated with markets, and some were located on rivers or roads that gave them good access to the coast.[54] There were, for example, over thirty on the Thames, and several others, including Bardney, Crowland, *Medeshamstede*, and Bawsey were on rivers that drained into the Wash. Archaeological and coin evidence confirms that Bawsey (close to King's Lynn) had good contacts overseas, as did Brandon on the Little Ouse in Suffolk. There must also have been landing places that were not associated with a minster, like the havens on the coast of Lincolnshire that, according to Domesday Book, did not pay toll before the Norman Conquest.[55] One was probably at North Ferriby on the Humber, where early continental and Kentish coins have been found that suggest it was briefly a landing- or perhaps trading-place in the late seventh and early eighth centuries.[56]

The close association of minsters with commerce, most clearly seen in the eighth-century toll-privileges, is not surprising. John Blair has recently emphasized the important role of minsters in the economy of eighth-century England and argued that their demand for imported luxuries was a 'prime stimulus of economic growth'.[57] They could meet most of their needs for food and raw materials from their own estates or by trading surplus produce, but they needed imports to supply their workshops with, for example, silk and other fabrics for vestments and church furnishings, gems used in ornaments and book-bindings, and pigments needed for manuscript illumination. Most monks and nuns were members of aristocratic

[53] Campbell, *The Anglo-Saxon State*, 104–5.

[54] Blair, *The Church in Anglo-Saxon Society*, 256–61.

[55] Sawyer, 'Early fairs and markets', 63.

[56] Naylor, *An Archaeology of Trade*, 52; Astill, 'Towns and town hierarchies', 101.

[57] Blair, *The Church in Anglo-Saxon Society*, 261; Moreland, 'The significance of production', does not discuss the contribution of monasteries to England's productivity in the eighth century, but admits that it may have been important (pp. 103–4).

families, and many of them retained a taste for luxurious imports such as wine, spices, silk, fine pottery and glass beakers, garnets, amethysts, and other gems.[58] By the end of the eighth century there were at least 200 minsters, some of them very large, and their total demand for imports was great. Some were obtained as gifts, but most had to be paid for by exporting produce that was in demand on the Continent.

Most of this trade passed through the major *wics*. London was especially important as it controlled access to the Thames and its tributaries and to the bishopric of Worcester. However, the distribution of early eighth-century continental coins shows that some overseas traders by-passed them. Around 20 per cent of the 744 early sceattas that by 2000 were recorded as single finds in England were porcupines from the Rhine estuaries, but that average conceals significant variations. Michael Metcalf has shown that in east Kent, East Anglia, and most of Lincolnshire the proportion was close to the average, but in London and East Anglia it was only 11 or 12 per cent, while along the south coast, in Humberside, and in Yorkshire it reached 30 per cent.[59] This suggests that some Frisian traders travelled directly to ports or markets on or near the east coast to buy the produce they wanted. As many of these markets were in areas that were later important for sheep rearing, it is likely that the produce most in demand was wool, as cloth or clothing. This conclusion is supported by other concentrations of early porcupines in Dorset and the Cotswolds, where sheep farming was later especially important. The upper Thames and the Worcestershire Avon are what Metcalf calls 'hot-spots' with 40 and almost 50 per cent respectively. He asks, 'If money had been carried to those two districts from London or the lower Thames should not one have expected figures closer to

---

[58] Campbell, *The Anglo-Saxon State*, 96–104; Blair, *The Church in Anglo-Saxon Society*, 136–7, 203–4.
[59] Metcalf, 'Variations', 43.

11–12 *per cent?* A likely explanation is that Frisian merchants who travelled through London spent their money in the wool-producing areas. Three-quarters of the Aston Rowant hoard of 324 coins, deposited *c.*710 about 10 miles east of Oxford, were continental, showing that such coins could be taken far beyond the coast, probably by traders.[60]

Æthelweard's account of the first Viking attack on Wessex shows that traders could also be expected to land on the south coast elsewhere than in *Hamwic*. He reports that in the reign of Brihtric (786–802) the king's *exactor* Beaduheard was in Dorchester when he heard that three ships had landed. 'Thinking that they were merchants (*negotiatores*) rather than enemies he sped to the harbour (*portus*) with a few men and ordered them to be taken to the royal vill, but they killed him and his men.'[61]

Tolls on foreign trade, probably levied at 10 per cent as in Francia, were an important source of royal revenues. Charters show that the Mercian king Æthelbald took toll in London and that Eadberht II, king of East Kent (762–*c.*764) did the same at Fordwich and Sarre. There is no such evidence for *Hamwic*, Ipswich or *Eoforwic*, but there is no reason to doubt that royal agents demanded toll at all of them. Tolls were probably also levied on inland traffic throughout England. That certainly happened in Mercia; in 737–738 Æthelbald remitted tolls on a ship of Minster in Thanet throughout the Mercian kingdom, and tolls on salt from Droitwich were probably levied then as they were in the ninth century.[62] It is, therefore, not surprising that kings tried to control trade that by-passed the *wics*.

Coinage was potentially another valuable royal resource, but before 750 it was not a royal monopoly in England south of the Humber.[63] Coins then circulated freely between the English kingdoms and

---

[60] *MEC*, 152, 167; Metcalf, 'Variations', 47.

[61] Æthelweard iii.1, 26–7.

[62] S 87; Maddicott, 'London and Droitwich', 41–3.

[63] This and the following three paragraphs are mainly based on *MEC*, 155–204.

across the Channel. Moneyers doubtless produced coins for kings south of the Humber as they did in Northumbria, but such coins were not distinguished from those produced for others; kings were not named on them. It has been claimed that when the Mercian king Æthelbald gained control of London *c.*730, he issued coins with the legend *(De) Lundonia*, but this is doubtful as there are earlier coins with a similar inscription.[64] Moneyers were certainly producing coins in London, *Hamwic*, and Ipswich as well as York, but the Christian imagery of many sceattas suggests that they may have been produced in, or for, minsters.[65] The apparent regulation of the weight and fineness of the main types of both continental and English sceattas was probably achieved not by kings, but by moneyers responding to the needs of their customers, especially merchants.

In the first half of the eighth century, English coinage was complicated and is incompletely understood. Over a hundred different types and some twenty-five main series have been recognized, but contemporary imitations cause confusion.[66] The main developments are, however, reasonably clear. At the end of the seventh century a flood of sceattas imported from Frisia and the lower Rhineland greatly increased the number of coins in circulation in England, and for about 25 years provided silver for English sceattas. Coins had previously been produced only in Kent and London, and their circulation was limited to the south-east. Within about 10 years there were new mints in East Anglia, *Hamwic*, and elsewhere, and coins circulated in most parts of England except the south- and north-west (see Figure 8). By *c.*710 Frisian sceattas were lighter and after 725 fewer reached England. This reduction was not compensated by imports of Merovingian denarii.[67] The quality of English sceattas began to decline, by 750 the number of mints and types was greatly reduced,

[64] *MEC*, 178–9, 181, 186; Williams, 'Mercian coinage', 212.
[65] Gannon, *The Iconography*.
[66] Metcalf, *Thrymsas and Sceattas*, 297–302.
[67] Op den Velde et al., 'A survey of sceattas', 125; Metcalf, 'Betwixt sceattas', 18–20.

Figure 8. Map: Single finds of sceattas in England. (From Metcalf, 'Betwixt sceattas', fig. 10, p. 23.)

and most sceattas were lighter and debased. Single finds suggest that large numbers were still being used in the *wics* and markets until *c.*750, when the number found in these places, and elsewhere, dropped dramatically.[68] Despite this the few coins and artefacts of the later eighth and early ninth centuries found in the *wics* and other markets show that they continued to function until the early ninth century.

In the eighth century there were significant differences between the coinages north and south of the Humber. Northumbria has, indeed, been described as 'for a time the only kingdom in north Europe issuing an overtly royal coinage'.[69] Its first silver coins were produced, probably in York, by King Aldfrith (685–705) and the royal coinage was revived by Eadberht (738–758), whose brother, Egberht, archbishop of York, also issued coins. Their coins were a little heavier and had a higher silver standard than contemporary southern English coins.[70] Metcalf has argued that in the interval between Aldfrith and Eadberht the J series of sceattas, without legends, was produced in York.[71] Over twenty of Aldfrith's coins have been recorded; most were found in Northumbria, but others were distributed from Lincolnshire to *Hamwic*, and twenty-three have been found in Domburg. Eadberht's coinage was substantial but few of his or later Northumbrian sceattas have been found outside Northumbria. Coins were issued by several later Northumbrian kings and archbishops until the Danish conquest of York in 866/7, although in the ninth century they were heavily debased and are now normally called stycas.

The Frisian coinage probably stopped in the 750s when Pippin, who then ruled Frisia, including Dorestad, established royal control over the coinage and began to produce coins in his own

---

[68] Blackburn, 'Productive sites'.
[69] *MEC*, 158.
[70] Ibid., 173
[71] Metcalf, *Thrymsas and Sceattas*, 341–67.

name that were thinner and broader, but weighed much the same as the earliest sceattas.[72] His coins are rare. The reform was developed by his son Charlemagne, whose coinage was on a large scale. In southern England attempts to reform the coinage and bring it more openly under royal control began after the death of Æthelbald, king of Mercia, in 757. Pippin's reform must have been a powerful influence, but the process was begun c.760 by Beonna, king of the East Angles, who, following the example of the Northumbrian Eadberht, issued coins in his own name with the title *rex*. His first coins were 75 per cent fine but the supply of silver was inadequate to sustain that level and his last coins, issued a few years later, were only 25 per cent fine. After conquering the East Angles, Offa (757–796) began producing coins as king of the Mercians in London, Canterbury, and East Anglia, probably Ipswich, which like Pippin's were broader and thinner, heavier (1.3g), and finer (96 per cent) than earlier eighth-century coins.[73] This coinage was at first on a small scale, but in the 780s Offa began issuing a very much larger coinage with a great variety of designs of high artistic quality, some with remarkably fine 'portraits' (see Figure 9). Towards the end of his reign, probably in 792, he again increased the weight of his coins, to 1.45 g, a standard that his successors tried to maintain for some time. Offa's coins have been found in most parts of England, except Northumbria, reflecting his hegemony.[74] He clearly had a much larger supply of silver than his predecessors. Metcalf doubts that this was thanks to imported Frankish coins.[75] He argues that very few Carolingian coins have been found in England because trade between Francia and England was very limited, despite the evidence discussed

[72] MEC, 108, 204.

[73] Chick, *The Coinage of Offa*; Metcalf, 'Betwixt sceattas'; Naismith, 'The coinage of Offa revisited'.

[74] Chick, *The Coinage of Offa*, 20.

[75] 'Betwixt sceattas', 17–20.

Figure 9. Silver penny of Offa (757–96), Light coinage c.785–92/3, London mint, moneyer Eadhun. © Fitzwilliam Museum, Cambridge

above.[76] An alternative explanation is that under Offa the use of foreign coins was prohibited as effectively as it was after 973.[77] The few Carolingian and Islamic coins that have been found were probably brought by invading Vikings in the ninth century.[78] The flight of Frisian merchants from York in 773 shows that they were still active in England, and the fact that for almost 100 years most coins south of the Humber were produced in Canterbury, London, Rochester, and East Anglia supports the textual evidence that the lively trade with the Continent was mainly through ports between Quentovic and Dorestad.

[76] See also Story, *Carolingian Connections*, 243–55.

[77] Metcalf, *An Atlas*, 85–9.

[78] Naismith, '"Kufic" Coins' explains the main exceptions; Blackburn, 'The Viking winter camp at Torksey', 225–30.

England's prosperity in the late eighth and early ninth is abundantly demonstrated by the material remains discussed and illustrated in the catalogue of the British Museum's 1991 exhibition *The Making of England*.[79] Leslie Webster's comment that 'the impression given by the increasing quantities of fine metalwork datable to the later eighth and first half of the ninth century is of a relatively stable and prosperous society' applies equally to the other evidence reviewed in that catalogue.[80] The great wealth implied by the surviving remains is confirmed by contemporary descriptions of churches and their treasures.[81] For example, Alcuin, in his poem on *The Bishops, Kings and Saints of York* credits Archbishop Æthelberht (776/7–779/80) with raising a great altar in his cathedral and covering it with gold, silver, and jewels.[82]

> High above this altar he hung a chandelier,
> Which held three great vessels, each with nine tiers.
> At the altar he erected the noble standard of the cross
> Covering it entirely with most precious metals.
> It was all on a grand scale and built on a lovely design,
> Weighing many pounds in pure silver.
> He erected another altar and covered it too
> With pure silver and precious stones,
> Dedicating it both to the martyrs and to the Cross.
> He ordered a large cruet to be made in pure gold
> And of great weight, from which the priest
> Celebrating holy mass could pour wine into the chalice.

The wealth of England attracted Vikings.[83] Their first reported raids were on Northumbrian monasteries: Lindisfarne 793, Jarrow 794, Hartness and Tynemouth 800. The royal minsters in Kent were also

[79] Webster and Backhouse (eds.), *The Making of England*.
[80] Ibid., 221.
[81] Dodwell, *Anglo-Saxon Art*.
[82] Ed. Godman, 118–19.
[83] For general surveys of the Vikings, see Sawyer, *Kings and Vikings*; Coupland, 'The Vikings in Frankia and Anglo-Saxon England'; Keynes, 'The Vikings in England'.

tempting and vulnerable targets, and by 792 Offa had organized defences in Kent against pagan seamen. Although the first recorded attack on Kent was on the Isle of Sheppey in 835, in 804 Lyminge minster was given a refuge in Canterbury; Minster in Thanet may have sought shelter there at the same time.[84] Kentish charters dated 811, 814, and 822 refer to the obligation to combat pagans and even to destroy their fortresses. In 800 Charlemagne organized defences along the coast north of the Seine, probably as far as the Rhine, against 'pirates who infest the Gallic Sea'. These defences were maintained and improved by Louis the Pious, and the first serious incursion was in 834 when Vikings, taking advantage of a dispute between Louis and his eldest son, Lothar, pillaged Dorestad. After that success the scale and extent of Viking incursions increased dramatically.

The Vikings caused justifiable alarm, but cross-Channel trade was not seriously affected until the 840s. Simon Coupland's re-examination of the coins found in Dorestad or minted there indicates that it enjoyed 'a sustained economic boom from c.795 to c.840'.[85] In contrast, archaeological evidence suggests that by 800 *Lundenwic* had begun to decline and that it was abandoned by the mid-ninth century.[86] Coin evidence confirms this: in the ninth century the number of London moneyers dropped fairly quickly. After c.820 London coins are exceedingly rare, and for about 10 years after 830 no coins were produced there, whereas the number of moneyers working at Canterbury and, after c.810, Rochester increased from about six to twelve by 845.[87] London's decline was mainly caused by the West Saxon conquest of Kent, Essex, and Surrey in 825. For about 20 years the Mercians were cut off from their main source of new wealth and their kings were weakened. This led to the disintegration of the Mercian regime in the early 820s,[88] while the West Saxon kings were not only

---

[84] Kelly, *Charters of St Augustine's*, xxviii–xxix.
[85] Coupland, 'Dorestad'.
[86] Cowie, 'Mercian London', 207.
[87] Blackburn, 'Alfred's coinage reforms'.
[88] Keynes, 'King Alfred and the Mercians', 3–4.

able to exploit the very rich Kentish minsters but could also profit from the trade that continued to pass through Kentish harbours.

Vikings raided the Isle of Sheppey in 835, and in the next 6 years south-west England was attacked at least three times, but the first major assaults were in 841 on Kent, East Anglia, and Lindsey, and in 842 when London, Rochester, and *Hamwic* were attacked. As a result the kings of Wessex and Mercia, Æthelwulf and Berhtwulf, began to collaborate. This enabled Berhtwulf to produce coins in London with dies supplied from Rochester.[89] Moreover, in 844–845 Berhtwulf confirmed Æthelbald's charter, dated 733, granting the bishop and community of Rochester remission of toll on one ship in the *portus* of London. This suggests that Æthelwulf may have allowed some revival of London's cross-Channel trade.[90] If so, it did not last long. In 850 Vikings wintered on Thanet, closing the Wantsum Channel and threatening traffic through the Thames estuary, and in 851 a large army stormed Canterbury and London, putting Berhtwulf and his army to flight. Although Æthelwulf defeated the invaders at *Acleah*, severe damage had been done; London produced very few coins for the next 10 years and the West-Saxon coinage may have been interrupted for a short while.[91]

In the 850s there were frequent raids with Kent and the Thames valley as favoured targets, and collaboration between the West Saxons and Mercians grew closer. Between 865 and 874 an alliance of Viking armies, mostly Danish, conquered southern Northumbria, East Anglia, and much of eastern Mercia, but not London, although they occupied the city during the winter of 871–872. Alfred successfully resisted attempts to conquer Wessex, and after defeating a Danish army at Edington in Wiltshire in 878, its leader, Guthrum, submitted and withdrew to East Anglia where he became

---

[89] *MEC*, 291–3.
[90] S 88.
[91] *MEC*, 290, 310; Dolley and Skaare, 'The coinage of Æthelwulf', 73.

king in 880. In Northumbria, and perhaps elsewhere, the Danish conquerors at first recognized English rulers under their authority but by c.880 all the conquered territories were ruled by Danes, and in some the invaders had begun to settle. The later term 'Danelaw' will be used here to distinguish the parts of England ruled by Danes in the late ninth and early tenth centuries, from the parts that remained under English rule.

Large quantities of treasure, coins, and bullion that the Vikings had obtained in Francia as well as England were taken to the Danelaw, and the wealth accumulated there was increased in 896 when an army that had invaded England 4 years earlier in the hope of extending Scandinavian conquests accepted defeat and dispersed. The *Anglo Saxon Chronicle* reports that some went into East Anglia and Northumbria, 'and those that were moneyless (*feohleas*) got themselves ships and went south across the sea to the Seine'.[92] The chronicler clearly believed, or claimed, that the first generation of settlers were only prepared to welcome newcomers who brought new wealth.

In the middle decades of the century, the coinages of Mercia and Wessex were progressively debased and by 870 their silver content was only 20 per cent. This was partly due to Viking exactions that reduced the amount of silver outside the Danelaw, but there was also a general shortage of silver in western Europe which caused a debasement of the Frankish coinage after 840.[93] In 875 Alfred, with the agreement of Ceolwulf II, undertook a major recoinage, issuing a new type that had five times as much silver as the coins they replaced. This was an astonishing demonstration of royal authority at a time

[92] Spufford, *Money and its Use*, 61 n. 5, claimed that this was a 'forced interpretation of the word ... rather than the more usual "without stock"'. Bosworth and Toller, *An Anglo-Saxon Dictionary*, translate it as 'moneyless' and record only one other occurrence, in Beowulf.

[93] Metcalf and Northover, 'Coinage alloy'; Blackburn, 'Alfred's coinage reforms', 202, 205.

of very great difficulty.[94] After Ceolwulf's death, probably in 879, Alfred had sole control of the London mint and undertook another recoinage, raising the weight of his coins to 1.6 g, which remained the theoretical standard outside the Danelaw for almost 100 years (see Figure 10). The number of coins circulating in Alfred's kingdom and 'English' Mercia must have been greatly reduced after 875, but they were much more valuable than recent issues.

Alfred's reform of the coinage was for the purposes of his government, not commerce. It manifested his control of London and his claim to be *rex Anglorum*. The new coins increased his revenues from traditional dues, rents, taxes, and legal penalties. In the second half of the century there were large fluctuations in the number of moneyers at Canterbury and London.[95] They do not, however, reflect the productivity of those mints. Mark Blackburn has noted that 'the evidence of single finds suggests that the size of the currency may have been stable or even declining in this period', and has pointed out that 'by merely relaxing the quota on the number of moneyers allowed at the mints, the king could have increased his revenue from fixed fees and the supply of dies'.[96] He has, however, argued that the increase in the number of moneyers in London from one to some thirty was due to economic expansion. This is most unlikely. There was little cross-Channel trade by then and *Lundenwic* had been abandoned. Any trade that passed through London was regional, mostly with the Thames valley, and was on a small scale until the early tenth century.[97] The fate of the *wics* shows that trade between England and its

---

[94] Nelson, 'Wealth and wisdom', has compared Alfred's recoinage with one made by Charlemagne in 793 or 794 and suggested that both were made at times of crisis to ensure that coins would be acceptable to their supporters as reward for loyal service. She believed that Alfred's recoinage was made possible by his victory in 878, but it is now clear that it was made earlier, *c.*875; Blackburn, 'The London mint'.

[95] *MEC*, 309.

[96] Blackburn, 'Alfred's coinage reforms', 204.

[97] Blackmore, 'Aspects of trade and exchange'. For London in the late ninth century, see Keene, 'Alfred and London'.

Figure 10. Silver penny of Alfred (871–899), London monogram type *c.*880. © Fitzwilliam Museum, Cambridge

continental neighbours declined dramatically in the second half of the ninth century. Ipswich survived as a centre of local, not long-distance trade; the latest evidence of contact with the Continent is a barrel used to line a well, which was made of wood from the Black Forest felled soon after 873.[98]

There was, however, some trade with Italy *c.*900. An account of the working of the royal treasury at Pavia, compiled in the early eleventh century, incorporates a text written about 100 years earlier concerning English traders.[99] It describes violent disputes between them

[98] Wade, 'Ipswich', 255.
[99] Brühle and Violante, *Die Honorantie Civitatis Pavie*; McCormick, *Origins*, 679–80; Pelteret, *Slavery*, 74–5.

and Lombard customs officials that led the king of the Lombards and the 'king of the Angles and Saxons', a title first used by Alfred in the 880s and later by his son Edward, to make a treaty.[100] Under this agreement English merchants were exempted from paying toll (*decima*) when entering Lombardy, and in return the English agreed to pay every 3 years to the treasury in Pavia 50 lb of refined silver, two large greyhounds with collars covered with gilded plate with the arms of the Lombard king, two shields, and the same number of lances and swords. In addition, the master of the treasury was to be paid 2 lb of silver and two large, fur-trimmed cloaks. This shows that the English were exporting dogs, weapons, and cloaks. The text also lists imports across the Alps on which toll was levied, but this cannot be taken as evidence for English exports in the tenth century; with the possible exception of tin, all could have been obtained elsewhere. The size of the triennial fee agreed by the English king suggests that English trade with Italy was on a very small scale at that time.[101] Fifty pounds was a tiny amount compared with the quantity imported into England in the eighth and early ninth centuries. By 900 very little new silver was reaching England, a change that is reflected in the English coinage after Alfred's death, which is discussed in the next chapter.

---

[100] Keynes and Lapidge, *Alfred the Great*, 227–8. Pelteret, *Slavery*, 75, gives reasons for thinking that the treaty was made in Alfred's reign.
[101] Southern, *The Making of the Middle Ages*, 43–4.

5

From Edward the Elder to Edward the Confessor (899–1066)

The decline of cross-Channel trade in the late ninth century meant that at the beginning of his reign Edward the Elder had a very limited supply of new silver. The evidence of single finds suggests that in the first half of the tenth century there were relatively few coins in circulation south of the Humber (Figure 7).[1] Only thirty moneyers are named on Edward's coins before 910 and they were not all working at the same time; seventeen of them had struck coins for Alfred.[2] With one exception, Bath, mints are not named on Edward's coins, but a number can be identified and there are good reasons for thinking that until 910 there were fewer than ten. Winchester was the most important. Canterbury and London, which had supplied almost all English coins in the ninth century, produced few, if any, for about 5 years. The Mercian mints at Shrewsbury, Chester, and Gloucester may have obtained new silver from Wales, but the others largely depended on the metal from coins withdrawn from circulation by taxation, rents, and other dues collected by royal agents. The king himself had a substantial treasure, but needed to make gifts and pay

---

[1] Blackburn, '"Productive" sites', 32.
[2] Lyon, 'The coinage of Edward the Elder', summarizing the more detailed discussion in CTCE, 20–96.

tributes or ransoms. Alfred's bequests of cash amounted to almost half a million coins, almost £2000, including £500 each to Edward and his brother Æthelweard.[3]

In contrast, by the end of the ninth century many coins of good quality were being produced and, to judge by hoards and single finds, were circulating widely in the Danelaw where there was, in Mark Blackburn's words, 'an organized monetary system, from which non-local coin was effectively excluded'.[4] Between c.895 and c.905 a large royal coinage was issued in York. At the same time, and for another decade, a large anonymous coinage naming the East Anglian king Edmund, killed in 869, was produced by at least seventy moneyers, most of them working in East Anglia, although some produced coins in the East Midlands. Estimates based on the dies used to produce coins in York when it was controlled by Scandinavians suggest that the annual output then often equalled or exceeded 'that of the mint in the prosperous eleventh century when York ranked as the second or third mint in the country'.[5] The contrast between the Danelaw and the rest of England in the early tenth century is confirmed by the single coin finds (see Table 1). The wealth of the Danelaw is also manifested by the seventeen silver hoards that are so far known from the Scandinavian kingdom of York, which, with one exception, were deposited before it submitted to Athelstan in 927. The largest by far, deposited c.905, was found in 1840 at Cuerdale by the river Ribble in Lancashire. It contained about 40 kg of silver, including c.7500 coins (5000 from the Danish conquests in Northumbria, East Anglia, and the Midlands, 1000 Anglo-Saxon, mostly of Alfred, 1000 from the Frankish Empire, mainly loot from raids in the Loire valley in the 890s and the Rhine–Meuse region in 902, and

[3] S 1507; Keynes and Lapidge, *Alfred*, 173–8, 313–26.
[4] Blackburn, 'Expansion and control', 134; id., 'Currency under the Vikings', part 2; *CTCE*, 97–107.
[5] Blackburn, 'The coinage of Scandinavian York', 302.

88

500 Islamic dirhams), 100 ingots, rings, rods, and fragments of brooches and other jewellery.[6] The contents of the other, much smaller, hoards were similar. For example, one found near Harrogate in Yorkshire in 2007 that was deposited in 927/8 contained sixty-seven pieces of silver (five arm-rings and fragments of brooches), 617 coins, mostly of English kings (Alfred, Edward the Elder, and Athelstan), some of Scandinavian rulers in the Danelaw, a few Carolingian deniers, and Islamic dirhams. It was, however, unusual in having a gold arm-ring and was packed in a fine Carolingian silver-gilt bowl.[7]

The relatively abundant and widely distributed coinage made possible by Viking loot stimulated the Danelaw economy. Craftsmen were encouraged to make pottery, wooden vessels, shoes, combs, brooches, and many other things for sale. Their activity was mainly concentrated in or near the centres of Danish power where potential customers were most likely to be found.[8]

The best evidence for this early development of the Danelaw economy comes from York.[9] Outside the Roman walls, areas that had been deserted since the fifth century began to be reoccupied. It has been shown that one modern street, Coppergate, was originally laid out in the early tenth century. Excavation of a small area has revealed four tenements fronting on it with boundaries that lasted for over 1000 years. Debris from many crafts was found there, including abundant evidence of metal working. Finds that are valuable as dating evidence are two obverse coin dies, one for a type of penny that was produced in York between c.910 and 927, the other for a York penny of Athelstan.[10] Similar urban developments in the early tenth century with new streets, workshops, and houses have been found in

---

[6] Graham-Campbell (ed.), *Viking Treasure from the North-West*.

[7] Williams and Ager, *The Vale of York Hoard*. I am indebted to Jane Kershaw for advice on the hoard evidence.

[8] Kershaw, 'Culture and gender in the Danelaw'.

[9] Hall, 'Archaeological aspects'.

[10] *CTCE*, 246–7.

Table 1. Single finds of coins minted 880–954 found in the Danelaw and elsewhere in England, registered in EMC and the Portable Antiquities scheme by 7 February 2012

	Total	Viking	Anglo-Saxon	Kufic
Yorkshire	38	28	4	6
Hampshire	21	1	19	1
Kent	12	3	9	–
Worcestershire and Gloucestershire	6	1	5	–

Note: Outside Yorkshire all Viking coins were imitations of English types. I am indebted to Rory Naismith for this table.

Lincoln, Norwich, Stamford, and Thetford.[11] By 1066 these were some of the largest English towns thanks to the economic expansion that began in the 970s. The foundations of their urban growth were, however, laid when they were ruled by Danes.

The church contributed very little to the economy of the Danelaw before the mid-tenth century. The only cathedral was in York, and the few minsters that survived had little or no surplus.[12] Most of the markets indicated by the 'productive sites' discussed in Chapter 3 apparently ended in the ninth century, but finds of later coins and metal artefacts show that in the Danelaw some continued into the tenth century or later: for example, Brandon in Suffolk, Bawsey near King's Lynn in Norfolk, and two in the Lincolnshire Wolds, West Ravendale near Grimsby, and Alford south-east of Louth.[13] There may have been minsters at Brandon and Bawsey, as there were in Lincolnshire at Louth, Partney, and Threekingham, where markets

[11] Hinton, *Archaeology, Economy and Society*, 82–94; Sawyer, *Anglo-Saxon Lincolnshire*, 184–96; Carter, 'Anglo-Saxon origins of Norwich'; Davison, 'The late Saxon town of Thetford'.

[12] Blair, *The Church in Anglo-Saxon Society*, 311–23.

[13] Pestell and Ulmschneider, *Markets*, 29, 32, 112–14, 124–6, 131–2; Sawyer, *Anglo-Saxon Lincolnshire*, 66, 174–6, 252–8.

are recorded in Domesday Book.[14] It is also significant that Ipswich was the only major *wic* that survived the ninth century, although its international trade did not revive until the early eleventh century.

By 920 Edward, in collaboration with the Mercians, had conquered all the Danelaw south of the Humber except Lindsey, and 7 years later, when York submitted to Athelstan, the conquest was complete, although numismatic evidence suggests that their authority in the conquered territories was not as effective as elsewhere.[15] The treasure obtained during that conquest enabled them greatly to increase their coinage. After *c.*915 Edward had well over a hundred moneyers, and at least twenty-seven of them who were in the Danelaw must have had as one of their main tasks the replacement of the Danish coinage by Edward's. Mints as well as moneyers were named on many of Athelstan's coins, but not those from the East Midlands. It is, however, possible to identify thirty-five mints. The fact that eighty of the moneyers named on his coins also struck coins for Edward, together with similarities of style, is good evidence that half of Athelstan's named mints were already established in Edward's reign (see Figure 11).

Although the number of moneyers is not a direct guide to mint output, there is no good reason to doubt that Athelstan's mints with more than five moneyers (Chester, Derby, London, Norwich, Oxford, Shrewsbury, and Winchester), together with York, were the most productive of the named mints. York is exceptional. Only one moneyer, Regnald, is named on its mint-signed coins. It is, however, likely that he had a monopoly of minting rights north of the Humber. Christopher Blunt, in his fundamental study of Athelstan's coinage, pointed out that the issue naming Regnald was substantial:

(the coins are plentiful and present great variety) ... it is apparent that so large a volume of coinage would at any other mint have appeared over the names of a number of moneyers. There are ample signs, moreover,

---

[14] Blair, *The Church in Anglo-Saxon Society*, 206–12; Darby, *Domesday England*, 369–70.

[15] Blunt, ' The coinage of Athelstan', 80; *CTCE*, 53 109, 208, 266.

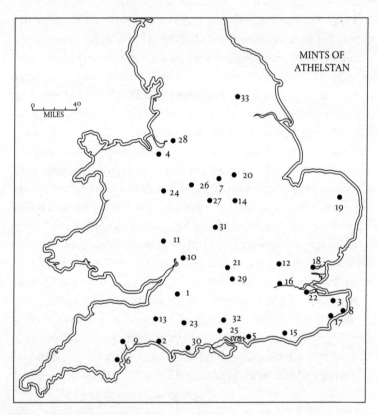

Figure 11. Mints of Athelstan

Mints of Athelstan

Map from Blunt, 'The coinage of Athelstan', 43 'Mints of Athelstan', renumbered alphabetically. Numbers of moneyers from *CTCE*, 260–3. Mints active in Alfred's reign are indicated by an asterisk, see Blackburn, 'Alfred's coinage reforms', 207–8.

New	Mint	No. of moneyers named on Athelstan's coins
1	Bath	2
2	Bridport	1
3	Canterbury*	5
4	Chester*	26
5	Chichester	1
6	'Darent' (? Totnes)	1
7	Derby	9
8	Dover	1
9	Exeter*	2
10	Gloucester*	1
11	Hereford	2
12	Hertford	1
13	Langport	2
14	Leicester	1
15	Lewes	2
16	London*	15
17	Lymne	1
18	Maldon	1
19	Norwich	8
20	Nottingham	2
21	Oxford*	8
22	Rochester*	1
23	Shaftesbury	2
24	Shrewsbury	9
	'Smrierl' (unidentified)	1
25	Southampton	2
26	Stafford	3
27	Tamworth	1
28	Thelwall?	1
29	Wallingford	2
30	Wareham	2
31	Warwick	1?
	Weardburh (unlocated)	1
32	Winchester*	8
33	York	1 (see text at note 17)

of an elaborate system of 'privy-marking' on Regnald's coins, such as could have been used to control the use of dies by individual workmen…which point to deliberate markings for the purpose of identifying the use of the die from which the coin was struck.[16]

The productivity of a mint was limited by the amount of silver available to the moneyers. Little silver was imported into England in the first half of the tenth century; cross-Channel trade was then on a very small scale—few if any imports of that period have been found in London or Ipswich. It has been suggested that the mints near the south coast, from Kent to Devon, 'were presumably located at or near the most significant ports for cross Channel trade'.[17] They cannot, however, have contributed much to England's store of silver. Some may have been imported from Wales, and the lead mines in the Peak District may have contributed a little, but the main source in the reigns of Edward and Athelstan must have been coins and treasure from the Danelaw, much of which was processed in Chester, Derby, Norwich, and York, as well as Lincoln, Stamford, and other unnamed mints in the East Midlands. It is likely that some of the treasure won during the conquest of the Danelaw was used to supply mints in other parts of England, especially the main centres of royal authority—Winchester, London, and Canterbury. Coins and treasure, some of it gold, from the Danelaw greatly increased the wealth of English kings. Eadred, who died in 955, was able to bequeath far more silver and gold in his will than his grandfather Alfred did.[18] According to William of Malmesbury, Athelstan distributed all the large booty he seized in York among his men.[19] That is unlikely, but there is no doubt that the conquest of the Danelaw enriched the warriors and agents of kings, from ealdormen and bishops to thegns and reeves. The heriots

---

[16] Blunt, 'The coinage of Athelstan', 89.
[17] Blackburn, 'Mints, *burhs* and the Grately code', 165.
[18] S 1507 and 1515.
[19] William of Malmesbury, *De Gestis Regum Anglorum*, ed. Stubbs, i. 148.

recorded in tenth-century wills show that Eadred and Edgar increased the equipment of their warriors.[20] They also show that many people, not only ealdormen, were able to bequeath much more silver and gold than King Alfred's ealdorman Alfred could.[21]

Outside the Danelaw the urban revival that gathered pace in the second half of the tenth century began with the royal *burhs*, established by Alfred and his children Edward and Æthelflæd to counter Danish invaders. Some were small forts that were soon abandoned, but most eventually became towns that are described in Domesday Book. This was, however, a slow process.[22] It may be that they were from the first intended to house permanent urban communities, but initially space was needed to provide refuge for local people when Danish raids were threatened.[23]

The account of the network of *burhs* in the south known as the Burghal Hidage lists thirty with the assessment, in hides, assigned to maintain and man each of them.[24] Each hide was to provide one man, and four men were needed for each pole (5½ yards) of rampart. The numbers ranged from a few hundred to 2400 hides for the largest (Winchester and Wallingford). Excavation has shown that they normally had an internal grid of streets, connected with one running behind the ramparts that enabled defenders to move quickly to where they were most needed. It is, however, misleading to describe these defenders as garrisons; most were not permanent residents but were summoned from the tributary estates when needed. Until the second half of the tenth century the *burhs* were not densely occupied. The blocks of land between the streets were occupied by large open properties that have been described as 'resembling farmsteads rather than town houses'.[25] There was a royal palace or cathedral and bishop's

---

[20] Brooks, 'Arms, status and warfare'.

[21] Whitelock, *Anglo-Saxon Wills*; S 1508.

[22] Loyn, *Anglo-Saxon England*, 136; Blair, *The Church in Anglo-Saxon Society*, 334.

[23] Keynes and Lapidge, *Alfred the Great*, 25.

[24] Ibid., 193–4, 339–41; Robertson, *Anglo-Saxon Charters*, 246–9, 494–6.

[25] Blair, 'Towns', 451.

residence in some *burhs* and in many there was at least one minster. Other residents were royal agents and local lords, some of whom had private churches. After 950 many of these large properties began to be subdivided into the narrow tenements characteristic of later towns.[26] Until then the *burhs* were predominantly centres of royal authority and aristocratic influence. It is not surprising that some craftsmen and women were employed to supply the needs of high-status residents, but there were no concentrations of craft workshops of the kind that flourished in the Danelaw towns. Until the mid-tenth century there is little evidence of pottery manufacture in English *burhs*, and although the technique of producing high-quality wheel-thrown pottery spread rapidly in the Danelaw, it spread very slowly elsewhere.[27]

In an important analysis of urban development in Anglo-Saxon England, Greville Astill drew attention to the contrasts between early tenth-century towns in the Danelaw and in other parts of England. He suggested that they may have been due to a 'dramatic reorientation of trade from the traditional regions of the Low Countries and the Rhineland to the Scandinavian kingdoms across the North and Irish Seas'.[28] There were certainly contacts between the Danelaw and Scandinavia throughout the tenth century.[29] There was probably some trade, for example in furs, but it cannot have been on a scale large enough to explain the development of the Danelaw towns.[30] There is good evidence of trade with Norway from the eleventh century, but the main medieval Norwegian export was stock-fish (wind-dried cod), which was an important source of winter and spring food in English towns.[31] Fish-bones from archaeological excavations in England show that the

---

[26] Biddle and Keene, *Winchester*, 340–4, 375–8; Baker and Holt, 'The city of Worcester'. In Oxford this development was in the eleventh century; Blair, *Anglo-Saxon Oxfordshire*, 150–67.

[27] Vince, 'Forms, functions'.

[28] Astill, 'Towns and town hierarchies', 110; id., 'General survey', 37–8; Hinton, 'The large towns', 229–30.

[29] Kershaw, 'Culture and gender in the Danelaw'.

[30] Sawyer, 'Anglo-Scandinavian trade'.

[31] Sawyer, B. and P., *Medieval Scandinavia*, 153–9; Nedkvitne, 'Handelssjøfarten'.

large-scale development of cod-fishing did not begin until the late tenth century.[32] The main argument here is that the early development of towns in the Danelaw, and later in other parts of England, was mainly due to an abundance and wide distribution of silver coins and bullion.

From the outset all but the smallest *burhs* had markets, most of which existed before they were fortified. It is, for example, most unlikely that the market that figures in the late ninth-century charter concerning the division of revenues in Worcester after its fortification by Æthelred and Æthelflæd was new.[33] Soon after 900 many *burhs* began to be called ports, a word that originally meant 'harbour', but came to be used for places under royal control in which toll was gathered.[34] Edward's laws include the rule that 'no-one shall buy except in a port, but he shall have the witness of the port-reeve (*portgerefan*) or another trustworthy man'.[35] The main purpose of this law was to hinder the sale of stolen goods. It was modified by Athelstan, who limited the prohibition to goods worth over 20 pence (such as horses and cattle). The implication is that the sale of less valuable goods would not be penalized.[36] The clause ends 'or else with the witness of the reeves in a public meeting (*folcgemot*)', but that exception was later cancelled.[37] There is no doubt that there were many markets and fairs outside the *burhs*, some of them held near churches on Sundays. Athelstan's prohibition of Sunday markets is no more likely to have been effective than similar prohibitions in the eleventh century.[38] In the tenth century, the goods sold in these markets were mainly produced locally, with some specialized products, notably pottery and salt, that were distributed widely.[39]

---

[32] Barrett et al., 'Dark age economics'.

[33] S 223. Tait, *Medieval English Borough*, 19–21, argued that it was new, but that was before the close association of minsters and markets was recognized.

[34] Sawyer, 'Early fairs and markets', 157–9.

[35] I Edw 1.

[36] II As 12.

[37] VI As 10; Wormald, *The Making of English Law*, 291, n. 130.

[38] Sawyer, 'Early fairs and markets', 65–6; Blair, *The Church in Anglo-Saxon Society*, 335.

[39] Dyer, 'Small places'.

The new mints established by Alfred were in *burhs*, and that remained royal policy, formally stated in Athelstan's Grately Code: 'no man shall mint money except in a port'.[40] This facilitated trade by providing cash when it was needed, but the mints and coinage served the purposes of royal government, not commerce. Taxes, legal penalties, and other dues, including tolls (for example, the wagon-shilling and load-penny rendered at Droitwich), were normally paid in coins, and they were used by kings and their agents to make purchases and gifts.[41] Coinage itself was a source of royal revenue by seigniorage (payments by moneyers for the right to strike coins) especially when the type, weight, or fineness were changed in a general recoinage.

As little new silver was imported before the 960s, mints had mainly to process silver that was already circulating or stored in England. There was, therefore, a gradual decline in the quality of English coinage, which accelerated in the first part of Edgar's reign.[42] Later in his reign there was a remarkable revival of cross-Channel trade which was mainly stimulated by a new abundance of silver in Germany that apparently began in the 960s, when Widukind reported that veins of silver were discovered in Saxony, probably in the Harz region.[43] That source was rich enough to enable Otto I to establish, or revive, a dozen mints, including Cologne and others in the Rhineland. Soon other sources of silver were discovered in Germany where, by the end of the century, there were at least eighty mints.[44] Many coins from these mints were exported to Scandinavia in the late tenth and early eleventh centuries.[45] Most were probably

[40] II As 13.

[41] S 223.

[42] *CTCE*, 235–45; Metcalf, 'The monetary history', 144–5.

[43] Widukind, III 63; cf. Thietmar, II 13; Spufford, *Money and its Use*, 74; Klappauf, Linke, and Brockner, 'Interdisziplinäre Untersuchungen'; Klappauf et al., *Schätze des Harzes*. Ehlers, 'Die Anfänge Goslars', casts doubt on the generally accepted identification of the source reported by Widukind as Rammelsberg.

[44] Spufford, *Money and its Use*, 74–7.

[45] Ilisch, 'German Viking-age coinage'.

used to buy furs, for which there was a vigorous demand in Germany; in the 1070s Adam of Bremen complained that 'we hanker after a marten-skin robe as much as for supreme happiness'.[46] These exports began c.950 but the main flood was after 990, perhaps because Scandinavia was then relatively stable, thanks to Svein Forkbeard.[47] This new German wealth stimulated economic expansion in the Rhineland and the Meuse valley, which in turn revived demand for English produce.

In the late eighth and early ninth centuries, the main port for trade between England and the Rhineland was Dorestad, but in the 840s it began to decline thanks to silting of the harbour caused by an eastward shift of the river's course, and by the 870s it was no longer a centre of international trade.[48] Its role was taken over by Tiel, about 10 km south-east on the Waal, another branch of the Rhine. There was then very little cross-Channel trade, but when it revived in the 960s Tiel's importance soon increased.[49] Excavations have shown that c.965 the trading quarter began to be rebuilt with large timber warehouses, and the harbour was reconstructed with a quay parallel with the river bank. About 20 years later it was replaced by piers, probably because of silting.[50] In 975 Otto II confirmed his father's grant to the Magdeburg merchants of freedom from imperial tolls throughout the empire, except at Tiel, Cologne, Mainz, and, in the east, Bardovic.[51] Tiel's main trade was with England, although this is not confirmed by texts until the early eleventh century. According to the *Miracula Sanctae Waldburgae Tielensia*, written c.1022, English merchants regularly visited Tiel, and in 1018, when Frisian rebels blocked

---

[46] *Gesta* iv. 18.

[47] Ilisch, 'German Viking-age coinage', 135; Sawyer, 'Swein Forkbeard and the historians'.

[48] Van Es and Verwers, *Excavations in Dorestad*, 1, 297–303; Coupland, 'Trading places', 220–6.

[49] Hatz, 'Tieler denare', 98–104; de Sturler, *Les relations politiques*, 135–9.

[50] Sarfatij, 'Tiel in succession to Dorestad'.

[51] *MGH, Diplomatum Regum et Imperatorum Germaniæ, Die Urkunden Otto des II*, no. 112.

access to the sea, Tiel's merchants demanded help from Henry II, arguing that if contact with England was broken, they would be unable to render their imperial dues.[52] They even required payment from other German merchants for the right to trade with England.[53] The importance of Anglo-German trade at the end of the tenth century is confirmed by the account of London's tolls that was probably made shortly before 1000, and is discussed below (p. 104).

German silver began to reach England before 973 but is not reflected in Edgar's pre-reform coinage. The authors of *Coins in Tenth-Century England* comment that the wide range of weights and variable debasement of that coinage 'points to a laxity, not to say a breakdown of control'. They add 'we cannot tell what caused it, though we think that the reform of *c*.973 would have been justified on these grounds alone'.[54] Imported silver facilitated that reform, which raised the weight and fineness of the coins, and made possible the huge increase of the coinage in the next two types.[55] Trace elements in Æthelred's coins confirm that they contain a substantial amount of new silver.[56] This is consistent with the equivalent reverse die estimates showing that, with the exception of Winchester, Exeter, and occasionally Chester, the seven most productive mints in his reign—Canterbury, London, Thetford, Norwich, Stamford, Lincoln, and York—were all on, or easily reached from, the east coast. They were, therefore, the most likely mints in which German silver, coins or bullion, was converted into English coins.[57] One result was that Æthelred and many of his subjects were much richer than their predecessors. The king was

[52] Alpertus, *De diversitate temporum*, 718.

[53] De Sturler, *Les relations politiques*, 139.

[54] *CTCE*, 265 and Tables 16, 18.

[55] The equivalent reverse die estimates, discussed in the Appendix, for the first three types after *c*.973 are: Reform Small Cross (*c*.973)—1031; Hand (*c*.979/80)—3235; Crux (*c*.989–*c*.996/7)—4072. Metcalf, 'Continuity and change', part 2, 78–85 (Appendix VI).

[56] Metcalf, 'The monetary history', 144–5.

[57] Together they produced over 50 per cent of each of the five types of Æthelred's coins. Metcalf, 'Continuity and change', 2, 72–9 (Appendix V).

able to increase the fighting equipment of his ealdormen and thegns, and wills show that they, and many others, were able to dispose of large amounts of gold and silver.[58] By the end of the century this greatly increased coinage was being widely distributed by traders as well as royal agents.

Among the many people of high status and low who must have welcomed this influx of silver, the monastic reformers encouraged by Edgar are prominent. They began their campaign in Winchester in 964 with the adoption of the Benedictine Rule by Old and New Minsters. In the next 10 years almost forty male communities and nunneries were reformed or revived.[59] This was a costly process. Churches had to be enlarged or replaced and made suitable for the monastic liturgy, and new buildings were needed to accommodate monks. Æthelwold, actively supported by Edgar, undertook a massive programme of rebuilding in Winchester.[60] Ely, *Medeshamstede* (later Peterborough), and Thorney needed complete restoration, a major task; it took 10 years to complete the buildings of Ramsey, a new foundation.[61] The contemporary lists of Æthelwold's gifts to Peterborough and the fuller record of the gifts made by Bishop Leofric (1046–1072) to Exeter Cathedral illustrate the church furnishings, vestments, and books needed by flourishing communities.[62]

Although the cost of building and equipping the reformed communities cannot be estimated, a little is known about the cost of endowing some of them with land. Several later texts based on tenth-century records of Ely, Peterborough, Ramsey, and Thorney show that Dunstan, Æthelwold, Oswald, and their supporters, clerical and lay, spent a great

[58] Whitelock, *Anglo-Saxon Wills*; Brooks, 'Arms, status and warfare'.
[59] Cubitt, 'The tenth-century Benedictine reform'; Barrow, 'The chronology'.
[60] Biddle, 'Felix Urbs Winthonia', 132–9.
[61] Keynes, 'Edgar, rex admirabilis', 44.
[62] Robertson, *Anglo-Saxon Charters*, 72–5, 226–31; Kelly, *Charters of Peterborough*, no. 30(a, b, c).

THE WEALTH OF ANGLO-SAXON ENGLAND

deal of silver and a surprising amount of gold to buy land for their monasteries. Barbara Yorke has suggested that Æthelwold must have paid several thousands of pounds to acquire estates, privileges, and works of art for his foundations.[63] He not only bought large estates, but also paid pennies for small parcels of land. For example, Peterborough's endowment included Barrow on Humber, the site of a seventh-century monastery, which he bought in 971 from King Edgar for 40 lb of pure silver and a golden cross which he valued more than the money.[64] It also included Wittering, a manor assessed in Domesday Book at 9 hides, which Æthelwold bought piecemeal in seven parcels, paying 12 gold mancuses and 2600 pence for five of them, amounting to 224 acres.[65] By such transactions a great deal of cash passed into circulation.

The abundant coinage stimulated the economy in many ways.[66] Landlords could collect rents in cash instead of kind. Craftworkers and small traders could employ labourers, carters, and others. Towns flourished.[67] Some large properties were subdivided into small tenements, and several expanded into suburbs.[68] Substantial landowners, thegns as well as nobles, found that it was advantageous to have houses in towns, normally in the same shire.[69] Cash was more frequently used in small as well as large markets; under Cnut purchases worth more than 4 pence required four trustworthy witnesses 'whether in boroughs or the country'.[70]

[63] Yorke, *Bishop Æthelwold*, 68–9.

[64] S 782; Kelly, *Charters of Peterborough*, no. 15.

[65] Robertson, *Anglo-Saxon Charters*, 78–81; Kelly, *Charters of Peterborough*, no. 30 (ix and xvi).

[66] Fleming, 'The new wealth', discusses the social and political effects of this abundant wealth which she suggests (p. 15) was based on grain, not wool.

[67] Astill, 'General survey', 38–42; Hinton, 'The large towns', 230–5; Blair, 'Small towns', 252–8.

[68] See above, pp. 24, 96.

[69] Fleming, 'Rural elites'; Blair, *Anglo-Saxon Oxfordshire*, 117–19; Hinton, 'The large towns', 233–4; Holt, 'Society and population', 81–2.

[70] II Cn 24.

The advantages of cash were widely recognized. This is neatly demonstrated by a colloquy composed by Ælfric Bata very early in the eleventh century for the instruction of novices, probably in Christ Church, Canterbury. It took the form of a discussion between a customer who hopes to commission a manuscript and a young monk who aspires to be a professional scribe.[71]

CUSTOMER: You, scribe, good sweet boy, I ask you humbly to write for me a sample (of your work) on a sheet or charter or a parchment scrap or in a diptych.

SCRIBE: Only if you wish to pay me.

CUSTOMER: Write me first a psalter or a hymnal or an epistolary or a troper or a missal or a travel book or a capitulary all properly laid out and arranged and accurately written and corrected, and I will pay you a good price, or I will purchase from you all these books and pay their price, either in gold or in silver or in horses or mares or cows or sheep or pigs or goats or clothing or in wine or honey or grain or vegetable produce.

SCRIBE: Nothing is more dear to me, than that you give me cash (*denarios*) since whoever has cash can acquire anything he wants.

CUSTOMER: You're already very wise.

SCRIBE: You're much smarter than me, who am a simple man.

CUSTOMER: Let's stop bantering like this. How much cash must I give you for one missal?

SCRIBE: You need to give me two pounds of pure silver if you wish to have it; if you don't want it, someone else will buy it. It costs a lot; but someone else would have to pay even more than you.

customer: Someone else may wish to be that stupid, but I don't; I wish to be cautious and buy your book at a fair price; and since my friends may tell me how much it's worth, let that be its price.

SCRIBE: How much do you wish to pay me?

CUSTOMER: Not as much as you said.

SCRIBE: Then how much *do* you want to pay, or how many silver pennies, or how many mancuses?

---

[71] Stevenson, *Early Scholastic Colloquies*, 50–1; Lapidge, 'Artistic and literary patronage', 143–5.

CUSTOMER: Believe me, I don't dare to give you more, nor to pay too dearly for it. Take this, if you wish; it's worth no more. I wish to give you twelve mancuses and count them out into your hand...

SCRIBE: Count out the coins here, so I may see what they're worth, and whether they're made of pure silver...[72]

This imaginary conversation would have been of little use as a teaching aid if the pupils were not familiar with cash as well as barter.

Cash also made it easier to import goods across the Channel or the Irish Sea. Exeter and Chester flourished and so did the beach market at Meols on Wirral, to judge by the large number of coins of Æthelred and Cnut found there.[73] Pottery found in London shows that by the early eleventh century it once again had an active trade across the Channel, especially with the Rhine and Meuse valleys. The pottery was apparently not itself traded, but was used on board ships visiting London.[74] Much more detailed information about this traffic is provided by a list of tolls levied on goods brought to London by ship during Æthelred's reign.[75] Some of the planks and cloth may have been English produce, but the list is mainly concerned with imports from the Continent. Merchants from Rouen who brought wine and *craspisce* (large fish, e.g. whales, porpoises) paid 6 shillings for a large ship and 'a twentieth part of the fish'. Unspecified goods were brought from Huy, Liège, Nivelles, Flanders, Ponthieu, Normandy, and Francia. Particular attention is paid to Germans, 'the men of the Emperor', who were especially privileged. The toll they paid at Christmas and Easter, three lengths of cloth, a large quantity (10 lb) of pepper and two saddle-kegs of vinegar, suggests that these were among the goods

[72] A mancus could be a gold coin worth 30 silver pennies or a unit of account for the same sum. Twelve mancuses amounted to 1½ pounds.

[73] Metcalf, *An Atlas*, 262.

[74] Vince and Jenner, 'The Saxon and early medieval pottery of London', 45.

[75] IV Atr 2; Keene, 'London', 191–2. Wormald, *The Making of English Law*, 328, 371, 443, discusses the character and date of this text.

they imported. They were also allowed to buy wool and *dissutum unctum* (melted fat, ?lard), and provision their ships with live pigs. These, the only exports specified, support Henry of Huntingdon's claim that the English earned silver from Germany by supplying fish, meat, cattle, and 'most precious wool'.[76] The importance of wool is underlined by Edgar's regulation of the price of a wey of wool at 120 pence.[77] The first explicit evidence for the export of English wool is in the account of the canons of Laon, who travelled to England in 1113 accompanied by Flemish merchants with 300 marks to buy wool. The report that the ship was attacked by pirates and that the merchants stored the wool they bought in a warehouse at Dover suggests that the trade was well established.[78]

The remarkable increase of English trade with the Continent and inland in the late tenth century was facilitated by the effectiveness of English royal government.[79] The king's peace protected markets and foreign merchants, and heavy penalties were imposed if it was broken.[80] According to Roger of Wendover, in 974 (or 969) Edgar severely punished the men of Thanet for robbing merchants from York.[81] A hierarchy of royal agents controlled the coinage, supervised markets, gathered tolls and taxes, and ensured good communications by maintaining roads and bridges and preventing hindrances to navigation on the main rivers.[82]

It is not surprising that there are more references to trade and traders after Edgar's reign than previously. The *Liber Eliensis* reports

[76] Henry of Huntingdon, *Historia Anglorum*, 5–6.

[77] III Edg 8.1–2. The earliest version penalized sale at a 'dearer' price, but later versions changed this to 'cheaper'. The intention may have been to encourage sale at first, and later to maintain the price.

[78] Herman, *De Miraculis S. Mariae Laudunensis*, ii. 4–5; Tatlock, 'The English journey'.

[79] Campbell, 'The late Anglo-Saxon state: a maximum view'; id., 'Was it infancy in England?'.

[80] Sawyer, *From Roman Britain*, 206–7, 226.

[81] *EHD*, no. 284.

[82] Campbell, 'Some agents and agencies'; Sawyer, *From Roman Britain*, 182, 230–1.

an incident involving Irish merchants in Cambridge, probably in Edgar's reign;[83] Æthelred's treaty with the Viking army in 994 shows that English merchants ships could be encountered in overseas ports;[84] and according to *Gethyncðo*, an early eleventh-century text, a trader who crossed the open sea at his own expense three times was entitled to the rights of a thegn.[85] The colloquium on trades and occupations produced by Ælfric of Eynsham, who taught Ælfric Bata, includes a section on merchants that is worth quoting in full:

MASTER: What do you say, merchant?

MERCHANT: I say that I am useful to both king and ealdormen, and to the wealthy and to all people.

MASTER: And how?

MERCHANT: I board my ship with my cargo and sail to lands overseas, and sell my goods, and buy precious things which are not produced in this country. And in great danger on the sea I bring them back to you here; and sometimes I suffer shipwreck with the loss of all my goods, scarcely escaping alive.

MASTER: What things do you bring us?

MERCHANT: Purple cloth and silks, precious jewels and gold, unusual clothes and spices, wine and oil, ivory and bronze, copper and tin, sulphur and glass and many similar things.

MASTER: Do you want to sell your goods here for just what you paid for them there?

MERCHANT: I don't want to. What would my labour benefit me then? I want to sell dearer here than I buy there so that I gain some profit, with which I may feed myself and my wife and my sons.[86]

Economic developments in late tenth-century England influenced the meaning of the OE adjective *rice*, a change carefully discussed by Malcolm Godden.[87] It originally meant 'powerful, mighty' and continued

---

[83] *Liber Eliensis*, 107.

[84] II Atr.

[85] Liebermann, *Gesetze*, 456–9 (trans. *EHD* no. 51a).

[86] Garmonsway, *Ælfric's Colloquy*, lines 149–166, trans. Swanton, *Anglo-Saxon Prose*, 111–12.

[87] Godden, 'Money, power and morality'.

to do so throughout the Middle Ages, but during the tenth century it began to be used to mean simply 'wealthy, opulent'. Ælfric, who wrote between c.990 and c.1010, frequently used it in that sense.[88] Godden's explanation for this semantic development is that 'it was a time when those in authority were conspicuously rich, and when their wealth seemed the most striking thing about those who were designated *rice*. Where wealth had formerly seemed a concomitant of greatness it now increasingly seemed the dominant characteristic.'[89] This is questionable. It is true that most of the examples of wealth gathered by Charles Dodwell are from the tenth and eleventh centuries, but that reflects the available evidence.[90] The gold ornaments and jewellery found in pagan graves and elsewhere, the great wealth of men such as Benedict Biscop and Wilfrid, and the condemnations of luxury by Bede, Boniface, and many others, do not suggest that the rulers and powerful men in Late Anglo-Saxon England were more conspicuously wealthy than their predecessors in the seventh and eighth centuries.[91]

A better explanation is that wealth had earlier been an attribute of power, but that by 1000 it was being acquired by merchants in expanding towns, as well as by traders 'who crossed the sea at their own expense', ceorls 'who prospered', and many others who were not powerful. This suggestion is supported by the similar development of German *reich* and French *riche*.[92] The economic development of England was closely linked with that of Germany. Ælfric's German contemporary Notker of St Gall frequently used *reich* meaning 'wealthy' in his translations.[93] The economic development of France was, however, slower. In the early eleventh century it was less urbanized than England

---

[88] Ibid., 51.

[89] Ibid., 54.

[90] Dodwell, *Anglo-Saxon Art*.

[91] Campbell, *The Anglo-Saxon State*, 55–106. Fleming, 'The new wealth', 3–15, accepts and elaborates Godden's interpretation.

[92] Ris, *Das Adjektiv* reich; Venckeleer, *Rollant*, 413–51.

[93] Ris, *Das Adjektiv*, 41–2. Götz, *Deutsch und Latein bei Notker*, 73, adds a few examples.

or Germany and its coinage was much poorer.[94] This was apparently the reason that *riche* only began to be used to mean 'wealthy, rich' in the twelfth century, especially in Anglo-Norman texts. Venckeleer argues that *riche* was first used in French to mean wealthy, independent of social status, in the mid-thirteenth century.[95]

England's wealth and the Anglo-German trade that sustained it soon attracted a new generation of Vikings. There were a few raids on Germany, but the most persistent attacks were on England. In the 980s the Anglo-Saxon Chronicle reports several raids, most in the west, probably by warriors from Dublin and other bases around the Irish Sea. The most severe threat was, however, posed by larger forces from Scandinavia, whose purpose was not to plunder vulnerable targets, but to cause such disruption that the English would pay large quantities of coins and treasure as tribute. According to the poem on the battle of Maldon, the raiders demanded gold rings and bracelets, and in 994 raiders were paid 22,000 pounds of gold and silver.[96] A few monasteries were plundered, but David Knowles concluded that 'there was no kind of general harrying and ravaging of the monasteries'.[97] The main targets were towns. Between 991 and 1016 the Anglo-Saxon Chronicle reports that Scandinavian raiders exacted tribute worth over 150,000 pounds.

Although minsters suffered little devastation, they had to sacrifice land and treasures. In 994 Archbishop Sigeric sold an estate of 30 hides at Risborough for 90 pounds of silver and 200 gold mancuses, i.e. 920 pence per hide.[98] That was a much higher price than was normal in the tenth century, when the price per hide (or sulung) was rarely over 300

[94] Johanek, 'Merchants, markets', 79–80; Keene, 'Towns and the growth of trade', 49–50; Grierson, *Coins of Medieval Europe*, 65–72.

[95] Venckeleer, *Rollant*, 442. I am indebted to Ian Short and Dieter Rosenthal for their generous help on this topic.

[96] Scragg, 'The Battle of Maldon', lines 29–35; *EHD*, 437–9.

[97] Knowles, *The Monastic Order*, 69–70. Cf. Gem, 'A recession', 41.

[98] S 882.

pence.[99] In 1005, when the threat was far more serious, the king sold a hide for 3000 pence.[100] Churches also had to sacrifice treasure, as Worcester did to pay the tribute demanded by Swein Forkbeard, when he conquered England in 1013. Richard Gem has drawn attention to Heming's report that 'on account of this very heavy tribute almost all the ornaments of this church were broken up; the altar panels, furnished with silver and gold, were stripped, ornamented books [and] chalices were destroyed, crosses were melted down'.[101]

According to Thietmar, in 1018 Cnut destroyed a fleet of thirty pirate ships.[102] After that there were no more serious raids until 1066, but as conqueror Cnut exacted a huge tribute, according to the Anglo-Saxon Chronicle £72,000 with £10,500 more from London. Cnut and his sons also continued to impose heregeld, an army tax introduced by Æthelred in 1012.[103] Cnut's first coinage, Quatrefoil, the largest before the Norman Conquest, suggests that in many parts of England there were reserves of silver—obsolete coins, ornaments or ingots—that were drawn on. Mints in the west, south-west, and Midlands produced many more coins of this type than before or afterwards, but the productivity of the largest, eastern, mints which apparently processed most imported silver did not increase on the same scale. This means that much of the silver needed to produce this huge coin issue came from local reserves.[104]

By the end of Æthelred's reign, payments of tribute to Scandinavian invaders led to a shortage of the silver needed to maintain the currency, and under Cnut the weight of the penny was reduced,

---

[99] S 500, 781, 866, 1216, 534, 545, 549,956, 677, 777, 781.
[100] S 910. Cf. S 903, 2 hides for the same price.
[101] Gem, 'A recession', 43, quoting Hearne, *Hemingi Chartularium Ecclesiæ Wigorniensis*, i. 248–9.
[102] Thietmar, viii. 7.
[103] Lawson, *Cnut*; Keynes, 'Heregeld'. The reliability of the Chronicle's information has been vigorously debated: Lawson,'The collection of Danegeld'; Gillingham, 'The most precious jewel'; Lawson, 'Those stories look true'; Gillingham, 'Chronicles and coins as evidence'; Lawson, 'Danegeld and Heregeld once more'.
[104] Metcalf, 'Can we believe'; id., 'Continuity and change', part 2, 63–4.

but not its value. The mean weight of Æthelred's coins ranged from 1.3 to 1.6 g. Under Cnut the range was 1.0–1.1 g and that level was maintained until c.1051 when the heregeld was abolished and the earlier standard was restored.[105]

The seven eastern mints that produced most of Æthelred's coins continued to strike at least 50 per cent of each type until c.1050, which suggests that Anglo-German trade, and silver imports probably continued at least until the Norman Conquest. It is not surprising that fewer dies were needed after Cnut's reign, for types were then changed more frequently. It is, however, remarkable that the average number of dies used each year in Winchester, York, and Lincoln during Edward the Confessor's reign were much the same as in Æthelred's (see Table 2). Domesday Book shows that the economy of Anglo-Saxon England was flourishing in 1065, and other evidence quoted at the end of Chapter 2 shows that by then many churches and some magnates had accumulated a great deal of treasure. It has, however, been claimed that relatively few coins were circulating in Edward's reign. According to Frank Barlow, for example, mintable silver was scarce and the king's cash receipts were so small that they could be kept under his bed.[106] Reasons for doubting the scarcity of silver coins in pre-Conquest England are discussed in the Appendix. Here it is sufficient to quote the evidence of single coin finds. These reflect the volume of the coinage and the frequency with which coins changed hands.[107] Martin Allen's analysis of single coin finds made in England and recorded by 1 April 2004 show that more coins were circulating in Edward's reign than at any other time in the eleventh century (see Table 5). This is consistent with the evidence of England's prosperity on the eve of the Norman Conquest, discussed in Chapter 2.

---

[105] Lyon, 'Some problems', 198–9.
[106] Barlow, *Edward the Confessor*, 157, 186; Metcalf, 'Continuity and change', part 1, 24.
[107] Above, pp. 57–8; Appendix at n. 18.

6

'Whoever has cash (denarios) can acquire anything he wants'

One of the main conclusions of this book is that the remarkable development of England's economy in the century before the Norman Conquest was due to its abundant and widely dispersed coinage, which was made possible by a flourishing export trade. The abundance of the currency and the scale of Anglo-German trade have both been questioned. Frank Barlow's claim that Edward the Confessor was short of cash has apparently been supported by Michael Metcalf's assertion that 'it seems safe to say that under Edward the Confessor there was a dramatic reduction in the size of the currency'.[1] The reliability of estimates of the size of the currency in the eleventh century is discussed in the Appendix, where it is argued that single coin finds show that more coins were circulating in Edward the Confessor's reign than in the next 70 years. James Bolton has dismissed my suggestion, made in 1965, that German silver was a possible source of English silver in the late tenth and early eleventh centuries as 'a very moot point indeed'.[2] I hope the evidence presented in Chapters 1, 5 and the Appendix will reduce the mootness of my suggestion.

---

[1] Metcalf, *An Atlas*, 74.
[2] Bolton, 'What is money?', 11.

The connection between economic development and a substantial, dispersed coinage is clearly demonstrated by the contrast between the Danelaw and the rest of England in the first half of the tenth century, discussed in Chapter 5.[3] Before the Scandinavian conquests there was only a similar abundance of coin in the first three or four decades of the eighth century when a huge quantity of sceattas from the lower Rhine region and Frisia were used to buy English produce. This influx of coins did not last long: by 725 it was greatly reduced. Cross-Channel trade continued, but until the tenth century it was mainly organized by or for rulers, magnates, and monasteries, who were, therefore, the main beneficiaries. Their success in acquiring treasure was clearly manifested by the Vikings who began to attack both England and Francia shortly before 800.

For most of its history Anglo-Saxon England was overshadowed by Francia, the source of most of its treasure. The contrast between England and France in the eleventh century is consequently remarkable.[4] The French king then had little authority outside the royal domain, a relatively small area in the heart of the kingdom. Elsewhere power was divided between a dozen great fiefs, including Flanders, Normandy, Anjou, and Burgundy, and many smaller ones. Philip Grierson's comments on French coinage in the eleventh century show how greatly it differed from that in contemporary England (see Figure 12a):

> Taken as a whole, it is one of the least attractive of the century, and indeed one of the least attractive in the whole history of France. The coins were mainly epigraphic...The rare figural types – a church, a bust, an angel, a key – are crude in design, and the general aspect and fabric of the coins are deplorable, with low relief, blundered inscriptions, distorted and illegible letters. The weights are in many cases infe-

---

[3] Strangely, Adriaan Verhulst says almost nothing about money or mints in his *The Rise of Cities in North-West Europe*.

[4] Campbell, 'Was it infancy in England?'; above, pp. 107–8.

rior to those of the preceding century, and there was a good deal of debasement.[5]

Coins were also scarce in many parts of France, for example Burgundy.[6] In 471 sales recorded in the archives of Cluny before 1050, almost half are for sums of 5 solidi or less and only five were for more than £5.[7] In the eleventh century the abbey of Cluny largely depended

a   b

Figure 12. a. Silver denier of the Abbey of St Médard, Soissons, eleventh century. b. Silver denar of Liutpold, archbishop of Mainz (1051–1059) with Henry III. © Fitwilliam Museum, Cambridge.

[5] Grierson, *Coins of Medieval Europe*, 68.
[6] Duby, *La société*, 348–63.
[7] Vigneron, 'La vente dans le mâconnais'

on the produce of its vast demesnes, for its annual cash income seems to have been about £300, while the cash income of Christ Church, Canterbury, under Archbishop Lanfranc was over £500.[8]

The explanation is apparently that in the later ninth and early tenth centuries there was a shortage of silver in western Europe, caused partly by the Vikings, and partly by the reduced productivity of the mines at Melle, the main source in Francia.[9] New sources were not discovered until the 960s, but these were east of the Rhine. Routes from most of France to the Rhine were overland, and traffic was hindered by tolls imposed by local lords. The English could reach the Rhine by crossing the North Sea. As Henry of Huntingdon reported, 'although little silver was mined in England, much was brought from Germany by the Rhine on account of England's wonderful fertility in fish and meat, in most precious wool, and in cattle without number. As a result, a larger supply of silver is found in England than in Germany.'[10] That was an exaggeration. Eleventh-century Germany had a very large number of coins, but they were not so well regulated as the English, and many were badly made (Figure 12b).[11] There is, however, no reason to doubt that the prosperity of Anglo-Saxon England was largely due to its 'wonderful fertility'.

---

[8] Duby, 'Le budget de l'Abbaye de Cluny'; see above, p. 11.

[9] Spufford, *Money and its Use*, 60–4; *MEC*, 235–40; Metcalf and Northover, 'Coinage alloys'.

[10] Henry, Archdeacon of Huntingdon, *Historia Anglorum*, 5–6.

[11] Grierson, *Coins of Medieval Europe*, 65–8.

Appendix: Estimating Dies, Coins, and Currency

The number of surviving coins or moneyers, when they are named, is not a reliable guide to the productivity of a mint. The number of dies used is a much better indicator; moneyers did not normally use more than they needed. Careful study of the surviving coins of a type can show how many dies were used to produce them in each mint, but most coins have not survived. However, if enough coins survive (normally at least twice as many as the recorded dies), it is possible to estimate the total number of dies used by using statistical formulae originally devised to study biological populations. Several problems have to be overcome. For example, the available coins should be a random sample, but that is rarely, if ever, true, and even if it were, the inevitably unequal output of the dies used means that they would not all have an equal chance of being represented in the surviving sample. Various formulae have been devised to counteract such uncertainties. They yield point estimates (sometimes misleadingly called 'central estimates') as well as a range of estimates within which there is a 95 per cent probability that the true answer lies. This means that the point estimates are not necessarily the most reliable. It is, therefore, desirable to give the upper and lower 95 per cent confidence limits as well as the point estimates, as in

Tables 3 and 4.[1] The reliability of the estimates depends on the accurate identification of dies. Numismatists do not always agree, but this is not thought to be a serious problem with most late Anglo-Saxon coin types.

Thanks to the large number of English coins surviving in Scandinavia for about 80 years after the reform of *c*.973, it is possible to make reasonable estimates of the number of dies used to make them. The first statistical analysis of a major mint was made by Stewart Lyon, based on the corpus of Lincoln coins compiled by Henry Mossop and published in 1970.[2] He estimated the proportion of the total output of each type issued from *c*.973 to 1066 that was produced by the known reverse dies.[3] Michael Metcalf subsequently calculated the total numbers of dies that these estimates would indicate if the average output of the unknown dies was the same as that of the known dies—a most unlikely situation, as he recognized, and he therefore called the result 'equivalent dies'.[4] He then made an ambitious and important attempt to estimate the number of dies used in all English mints between *c*.973 and the 1050s by combining the Lincoln estimates with the evidence of the 16,971 Anglo-Saxon coins of the period in the Stockholm and Copenhagen collections, most of which came from Scandinavian hoards. For example, it was estimated that 194 reverse dies were used at Lincoln to produce the last type of Cnut. As these coins constitute 13.5 per cent of that type in the Scandinavian collections, and on the assumption that the

[1] Stewart Lyon discusses the problems and possible solutions in 'Die-estimation'. For a brief summary of the results obtained for the Lincoln mint by different formulae, see the appendix he contributed to Metcalf, 'Continuity and change' part 2, 88–90. In 2006 Warren Esty published revised formulae in 'How to Estimate'. In a letter dated 18 April 2007 Stewart Lyon described Esty's approach as 'superior to my own methodology when the proportion of singleton dies (i.e. dies represented by only one coin in the sample) is high, which is often the case after Cnut's reign.'

[2] Henry Mossop, *The Lincoln Mint*, pp. 11–19 and Analytical Appendixes (unpaginated at the end of the book).

[3] Ibid., Appendix 4, Table 4.

[4] Michael Metcalf, 'Continuity and change' part 2, 52–3; cf. id., *An Atlas*, 22–4.

proportion of coinage from each mint exported to Scandinavia was equal, he argued that 1437 reverse dies were used to produce the whole issue, distributed among the mints in proportion to their representation in the Scandinavian sample.[5] These Lincoln estimates, adjusted in proportion to the respective numbers of coins of other types in the Scandinavian collections, have yielded the Lincoln-equivalent reverse die estimates listed by Metcalf in 1981.[6]

Stewart Lyon has calculated revised estimates for the Lincoln mint using Esty's new formulae.[7] The results, summarized in Table 3, show that until the reign of Edward the Confessor the new estimates are significantly higher than the earlier ones on which Metcalf based his estimates of equivalent reverse dies. This suggests that many of the equivalent reverse die estimates, which have been widely accepted, are too low.

It is now possible to test the reliability of the equivalent reverse die estimates for two major mints thanks to the corpora of Winchester and York coins prepared by Yvonne Harvey and William Lean respectively. Lyon has analysed this evidence using Esty's revised formulae and has generously supplied some of the results in advance of their publication (see Table 4).[8] This analysis shows that many of the equivalent reverse die estimates for these mints are close to, or under, the lower 95 per cent confidence limits of the new estimates. The

---

[5] For example, 5,09% of this type in the Scandinavian collections are from Winchester (Metcalf, 'Continuity and change' part 2, Appendix V 73). That percentage of the estimated national total of 1437 reverse dies gives 73 as the Lincoln-equivalent reverse die estimate for Winchester.

[6] Metcalf, 'Continuity and change' part 2, Appendix VI, 78–85. Alternative estimates, based not on equivalent dies but on ranges of point estimates for Lincoln developed by Lyon in 1981, 'Alternative estimates', and applied to the 34,707 coins listed by Petersson, *Anglo-Saxon Currency*, are reported by Allen, 'The volume of the English currency', 490–3 (Tables 3 and 4). Most are fairly close to the equivalent reverse die estimates, but for the last types of Edward the Confessor they are much larger. These estimates influenced Metcalf's discussion of mint productivity in Edward's reign. Metcalf, 'Continuity and change' part 2, 53–5 including Fig. 7, and Table 5 (p. 63).

[7] See note 1 above.

[8] Lyon, 'Minting in Winchester'.

main exceptions are that the equivalent reverse die estimates for the last four types of Æthelred's coins from Winchester and for the three types of Harald I and Harthacnut from York are all higher than Lyon's new upper 95 per cent confidence limits.[9]

Estimates of the number of dies used make it possible to compare the productivity of mints and to trace changes. It is, however, not possible to determine with any precision how many coins were produced. The number of coins struck by dies varied greatly. In small mints many dies were probably underused, but that is less likely in major ones. Metcalf made the cautious assumption that on average each die struck about 10,000 coins, but later mint records show that the figure was often much higher. For example, between 1281 and 1307 in the mints of London and Canterbury the average output per die used to strike pennies, halfpennies, and farthings was over 16,000 coins.[10] Martin Allen has recently suggested that a range of estimates using multiples of 10,000 and 20,000 per reverse die provide a more reliable guide to the number of coins produced.[11]

Estimates of the number of coins in circulation are even more uncertain. They depend on assumptions about the number exported by traders, by raiders, as the wages of foreigners serving the English king, or as gifts. Coins were also withdrawn from circulation by accidental losses and hoarding. Another significant uncertainty is how many coins were not reminted when a new type was issued.

---

[9] Stewart Lyon has explained, in a letter dated 12 June 2007, that the reason for Metcalf's higher equivalent die estimates is that he 'had to assume that the average number of coins surviving per known die in each type would be the same as at Lincoln for all other mints. The Winchester and York corpuses have shown that this assumption can be wide of the mark. For example, in the Winchester corpus the average number of coins per reverse die in Long Cross is 10, compared with 3½ at Lincoln, and this is because Winchester evidently ceased production of Long Cross after the first flush of minting in which a disproportionately large quantity of coins was exported to Scandinavia. So the point estimate for missing Lincoln dies is 68 compared with only 1 for Winchester.'

[10] Allen, 'Medieval English die-output'.

[11] Allen, 'The volume of the English currency', 489–90.

Metcalf has, nevertheless, boldly attempted to develop a model of the currency from c.973 to the 1050s, in which the number of coins in circulation during the currency of a type was never more than half, and sometimes less than a quarter, of the number produced.[12] It is, however, important to bear in mind Metcalf's own admission that his model involves a good deal of guesswork and that the results are largely speculative. All its elements have a wide margin of uncertainty and depend on assumptions, most of which cannot be tested. The inflows and outflows have largely been determined by the needs of the model, and some are improbable. It is, for example, difficult to accept that between the first major Scandinavian attack in 992 and the death of Cnut in 1035 trade accounted for the export of almost twice as many pennies (93 million) as Danegeld and Heregeld (53 million).

There have been several attempts to estimate the size of the English currency in the late 1080s, based on the known coins of the *Paxs* type that was current 1087–c. 1090?.[13] Nicholas Mayhew's 'guestimate' of £37,500 has been widely accepted.[14] Martin Allen has pointed out that this was Michael Dolley's very questionable calculation, made in 1960, on the assumption that 600 reverse dies each produced 15,000 coins.[15] Allen has himself very tentatively offered an alternative estimate of £30,000–£70,000 based on Michael Metcalf's 'best guess' that there were 600–880 reverse dies of *Paxs*.[16] He has, however, recently insisted that 'the continued use of precise estimates such as Dolley's without further qualification cannot be justified on the available evidence'.[17]

[12] Metcalf, 'Continuity and change' part 2, 62–5.

[13] Allen, *Mints and Money*, 319–21.

[14] 'Modelling medieval monetisation'; 'Coinage and money in England, c. 1086–c. 1500'; cf. Dyer, *Making a Living*, 98; Bolton, 'What is money?', 10; Britnell, 'Uses of money', 17.

[15] Dolley, *The Norman Conquest and the English Coinage*.

[16] Allen, 'The volume of the English currency, c.973–1158', 494.

[17] *Mints and Money*, 321.

Thanks to metal detector users, the growing number of single coin finds in England is a useful guide to the number of coins in circulation from time to time.[18] These finds are especially valuable as evidence for the size of the currency on the eve of the Norman Conquest. Metcalf's model apparently confirms Frank Barlow's judgement that in Edward the Confessor's reign mintable silver was scarce and the king's cash receipts were so small that they could be kept under his bed.[19] This is most unlikely. Martin Allen's analysis of the finds in England of coins produced between 973 and 1180 that were recorded by 1 April 2004, summarised in Table 5, suggests that more coins were circulating in Edward's reign than at any other time in the eleventh century, or indeed between 1066 and 1135.[20] This is consistent with the other evidence of England's prosperity TRE, discussed in Chapter 2.

Table 2. The average number of reverse dies used per year in Winchester, York, and Lincoln c.973–1066, based on the point estimates in Table 4

	Winchester	York	Lincoln
c.973–1016	24.5	34.1	30.9
1016–1035	28.5	45.6	50.9
1035–1042	33.7	26.3	57.1
1042–1066	25.6	32.0	28.4
c. 973–1066	26.3	35.3	36.3

[18] Blackburn, Znaleziska pojedyncze; id., ' "Productive" sites', 23, 34–5; Allen, *Money and Mints*, 319–20; Naismith, 'The English monetary economy, c. 973–1100'.

[19] Barlow, *Edward the Confessor*, 143–57, 186; cf. Metcalf, 'Continuity and change' part 1, 24.

[20] Allen, 'The volume of the English currency', 499–501; id., *Mints and Money*, 320.

Table 3. Estimates of the number of reverse dies used in the Lincoln mint, c.973–1066

	1970 (equivalent dies)	**2007 (actual dies)**
c.973–1016	1036	1112-1328-1629
1016–1035	791	874-968-1073
1035–1042	314	319-400-502
1042–1066	612	484-682-988

The 1970 figures were derived from Lyon's estimates of the proportion of the total output of each type that was minted from known reverse dies. The figures assume that the average output of known and unknown dies was the same, which is unlikely, so they are described as 'equivalent' rather than 'actual' dies.

The 2007 estimates have been calculated by Lyon from the same data but using a statistical technique devised by Warren Esty to allow for variation in die output. As well as an enhanced 'point' estimate in the middle of the range of probability, upper and lower limits are given within which the true number of dies used can be expected with 95 per cent confidence to lie if the data can be regarded as a random sample of the coinage. See also Lyon's note on 'Die analysis and estimation' in id., 'Minting in Winchester', 30.

The total estimates for each period in this and other tables in this appendix are the sum of the estimates for each type, given in Table 4. They obviously exclude types for which there are insufficient data and may therefore be understatements. It should be noted that totalling the confidence limits produces a range that may be wider than necessary because it makes no allowance for the possibility that, for the individual types, the true answers may lie on different sides of the point estimates.

Table 4. Estimates of the number of reverse dies used in Winchester, York, and Lincoln, c.973–1066

Lyon's estimates of the number of reverse dies used in the mints of Winchester, York, and Lincoln between c.973 and 1066, from Lyon, 'Minting in Winchester', compared with the Lincoln-equivalent die estimates for Types 1–16 from Metcalf, 'Continuity and Change', 2, Appendix VI (pp. 78–85) and for Lincoln types 17–23 from Lyon, 'Alternative estimates', formula 1.

A = number of coins; **B** = point-estimates and 95% confidence limits of actual dies, 2007;
C = Lincoln equivalent die-estimates.
The Type numbers are those proposed by Stewart, 'A numeration'.
i.d. = inadequate data.

See Table 3 for a cautionary note on the reliability of the total estimates.

Types	Winchester		
	A	B	C
1 Reform	35	57-95-162	130
2 A First Hand	94	165-220-293	237
2 B Second Hand	43	79-130-216	80
Benediction Hand	10	10-14-24	
3 Crux	219	263-283-304	317
4 Long Cross	34	34-35-37	76
5 Helmet	42	42-48-54	64
6 Last Small Cross	178	218-234-252	291
Edgar to Æthelred		866-1059-1342	
7 Quatrefoil	204	304-347-397	298
8 Pointed Helmet	82	97-108-119	98
9 Short Cross	63	75-87-101	73
Cnut		476-542-617	
10 Jewel Cross	40	46-66-94	40
11 Fleur de Lis	32	35-45-59	49
12 Arm and Sceptre	36	59-95-155	37
Harold I & Harthacnut		140-206-308	
13 Pacx	27	41-73-134	26
14 Radiate/Small Cross	29	38-56-85	25
15 Trefoil/Quadrilateral	24	38-68-128	25
16 Small Flan	28	i.d.	16

Winchester

Types	A	B	C
17 A Expanding Cross—Light	21	i.d.	
17 B Expanding Cross—Heavy	18	19-25-34	
18 Pointed Helmet	58	87-122-169	
19 Sovereign/Eagles	36	57-90-146	
20 Hammer Cross	33	40-57-81	
21 Facing Bust	17	19-30-49	
22 Pyramids	34	40-54-74	
23 Pax	14	20-36-70	
Edward Confessor & Harold II		400-611-970	

York

Types	A	B	C
1	79	169-252-378	87
2A	90	168-231-318	160
2B	1	i.d.	
3	203	360-430-513	383
4	139	171-185-200	153
5	107	138-156-177	151
6	164	196-214-234	253
		1202-1468-1820	
7	276	408-451-499	402
8	234	262-275-289	267
9	122	132-140-149	178
		802-866-937	
10	58	70-82-96	89
11	51	53-60-67	108
12	30	34-42-52	47
		157-184-215	
13	29	37-56-86	48

(Continued)

Table 4. Continued

Types	A	B	C
		York	
14	73	90-104-121	49
15	50	59-69-81	99
16	26	26-30-35	25
17A	46	55-67-82	
17B	30	33-42-53	
18	55	61-68-76	
19	48	i.d.	
20	67	73-82-92	
21	83	93-103-114	
22	41	42-46-51	
23	21	22-27-34	
		650-768-917	

Types	A	B	C
		Lincoln	
1	46	72-109-167	82
2A	33	60-106-194	77
2B	–	– – –	–
3	127	213-260-318	198
4	183	234-251-269	208
5	80	110-133-161	105
6	277	423-469-520	370
		1112-1328-1629	
7	276	425-478-538	378
8	186	242-265-290	219
9	175	207-225-245	194
		874-968-1073	
10	91	128-158-195	126
11	81	121-150-187	116

		Lincoln		
Types	A	B	C	
12	51	70-92-120	72	
		319-400-502		
13	52	79-109-151	81	
14	51	58-75-97	62	
15	59	84-112-150	88	
16	21	22-30-42	25	
17A	25	28-42-65	76	
17B	36	40-49-60		
18	34	48-73-111	56	
19	24	i.d.	73	
20	44	62-88-125	68	
21	24	33-56-98	42	
22	14	16-30-62	23	
23	14	14-18-27	16	
		484-682-988		

Table 5. Single coin finds recorded in EMC before 1 April 2004, from Allen, 'The volume of the English Currency', 498–500, and Appendix 1 (p. 502)

	Single finds	Finds per year
Æthelred 978–1016	315	8.3
Cnut 1016–1035	169	8.9
Harold I and Harthacnut 1035–1042	81	11.6
Edward and Harold II 1042–1066	321	13.4
William I 1066–1087	185 or 154	8.8 or 7.3[*]
William II 1087–1100	48 or 79	3.6 or 6.1[*]
Henry I 1100–1135	247	7.1

[*] Depending on whether Paxs is regarded as the last type of William I or the first of William II.

REFERENCES

Abdy, R. and Williams, G., 'A catalogue of hoards and single finds from the British Isles, *c.*410–675', in B. Cook and G. Williams (eds.), *Coinage and History* 11–73.

Adam of Bremen, *Gesta Hammaburgensis Ecclesie Pontificum*, ed. B. Schmeidler, MGH SRG (Hannover, 1917).

Æthelweard, *The Chronicle of Æthelweard*, ed. A. Campbell (London, 1962).

Alcuin, *Epistolae*, ed. E. Dümmler, MGH Epist. 4, Karolini Aevi 2 (Berlin, 1895).

—— *The Bishops, Kings and Saints of York*, ed. P. Godman (Oxford, 1982).

Allen, M., 'Medieval English die-output', *BNJ* 75 (2004), 39–49.

—— 'The volume of the English currency, *c.*973–1158', in B. Cook and G. Williams (eds.), *Coinage and History*, 487–523.

—— Silver production and the money supply in England and Wales, 1086–*c.*1500', *Economic History Review* 64 (2011), 114–31.

—— *Mints and Money* (Cambridge, 2012).

Allott, S., *Alcuin of York* (York, 1974).

Alpertus, *De diversitate temporum*, MGH SS iv. 700–23.

Anglo-Saxon Chronicle: ed. C. Plummer, *Two of the Saxon Chronicles Parallel*, 2 vols. (Oxford, 1892–9, reissued 1952); D. Whitelock with D. C. Douglas and S. I. Tucker, *The Anglo-Saxon Chronicle: A Revised Translation* (London, 1961).

Archer, S., 'Late Roman gold and silver hoards in Britain', in P. J. Casey (ed.), *The End of Roman Britain*, BAR British ser. 71 (Oxford, 1979), 29–64.

Arrhenius, B., *Merovingian Garnet Jewellery: Emergence and Social Implications* (Stockholm, 1985).

Astill, G., 'Towns and town hierarchies in Saxon England', *Oxford Journal of Archaeology* 10 (1991), 95–117.

—— 'General survey 600–1300', in *CUHB*, 17–49.

Attenborough, F. L., *The Laws of the Earliest English Kings* (Cambridge, 1922).

Baker, N. and Holt, R., 'The city of Worcester in the tenth century', in N. Brooks and C. Cubitt (eds.), *St Oswald of Worcester*, 129–46.

Baring, F. H., *Domesday Tables* (London, 1909).

Barlow, F., *Edward the Confessor* (London, 1970).

—— (ed. and trans.), *The Life of Edward who Rests at Westminster*, 2nd edn. (Oxford, 1992).

—— 'The Winton Domesday', in Biddle, *Winchester in the Early Middle Ages*, 1–141.

Barrett, J. H., Locker, A. M., and Roberts, C. M., '"Dark Age Economics" revisited: the English fish bone evidence AD 600–1600', *Antiquity* 78 (2004), 618–36.

Barrow, J., 'The chronology of the Benedictine reform', in D. Scragg (ed.), *Edgar*, 211–23.

Bassett, S. (ed.), *The Origins of Anglo-Saxon Kingdoms* (Leicester, 1989).

Baxter, S., 'The representation of lordship and land tenure in Domesday Book', in E. Hallam and D. Bates (eds.), *Domesday Book* (Stroud, 2001), 73–102.

Bede, *Opera: Venerabilis Bædæ Opera Historica*, ed. C. Plummer, 2 vols. (Oxford, 1896).

—— *Historia abbatum*, in Bede, *Opera* i. 364–87.

—— *Historia Ecclesiastica Gentis Anglorum*, in Bede, *Opera* i. 5–360; ed. and trans. B. Colgrave and R. A. B. Mynors, *Bede's Ecclesiastical History of the English People* (Oxford, 1996).

Biddle, M., '*Felix Urbs Winthonia*: Winchester in the age of monastic reform', in D. Parsons (ed.), *Tenth-Century Studies* (London and Chichester, 1975), 123–40.

—— 'Towns', in D. M. Wilson (ed.), *The Archaeology of Anglo-Saxon England* (London, 1976), 99–150.

—— (ed.), *Winchester in the Early Middle Ages: An Edition and Discussion of the Winton Domesday*, Winchester Studies 1 (Oxford, 1976).

—— 'Early Norman Winchester', in J. C. Holt (ed.), *Domesday Studies*, 311–31.

—— (ed.), *The Winchester Mint and Coins and Related Finds from the Excavations of 1961–71*, Winchester Studies 8 (Oxford, 2012).

—— and Keene, D. J., 'Winchester in the eleventh and twelfth centuries', in M. Biddle, (ed.), *Winchester in the Early Middle Ages*, 241–508.

Birch, W. de G. (ed.), *Cartularium Saxonicum*, 3 vols. (London, 1885–99).

Blackburn, M. A. S., 'The Welbourne (Lincs.) hoard 1980–82 of Æthelred II coins', *BNJ* 55 (1985), 79–83.

—— (ed.), *Anglo-Saxon Monetary History: Essays in Memory of Michael Dolley* (Leicester, 1986).

—— 'Znaleziska pojedyncze jako miara aktywnosci monetarnej we wczesnym sredniowieczu' (Single-finds as a measure of monetary activity in the Early Middle Ages), *Prace I materially. Museum Archaeologicznego i Etnografic-*

nznego w Lodzi. Seria numizmatyczna I konserwatorska 9 (1989), 67–85 (English summary).

—— 'Æthelred's coinage and the payment of tribute', in D. Scragg (ed.), *The Battle of Maldon AD 991* (Oxford, 1991), 156–69.

—— 'Coin circulation in Germany during the early middle ages: the evidence of single finds', in B. Kluge (ed.), *Fernhandel und Geldwirtschaft* (Sigmaringen, 1993), 37–54.

—— 'Money and coinage', *NCMH* ii, 538–59.

—— 'Mints, *burhs* and the Grately Code, cap. 14.2', in D. Hill and A. R. Rumble (eds.), *The Defence of Wessex: The Burghal Hidage and Anglo-Saxon Fortifications* (Manchester, 1996), 160–75.

—— 'Alfred's coinage reforms in context', in T. Reuter (ed.), *Alfred*, 199–217.

—— 'The coinage of Scandinavian York': repr. id., *Viking Coinage*, 281–307.

—— 'Currency under the Vikings, part 2: the two Scandinavian kingdoms of the Danelaw, *c.*895–954', repr. id., *Viking Coinages*, 32–57.

—— 'Expansion and control: aspects of Anglo-Saxon minting south of the Humber', in J. Graham-Campbell et al.,(eds.), *Vikings and the Danelaw*, 125–81. Repr. Blackburn, M., *Viking Coinage*, 149–66.

—— 'The London mint in the Reign of Alfred', in M. A. S. Blackburn and D. N. Dumville (eds.), *Kings, Currency*, 105–23.

—— ' "Productive" sites and the pattern of coin loss in England, 600–1180', in T. Pestell and K. Ulmschneider (eds.), *Markets in Early Medieval Europe*, 20–36.

—— 'Gold in England during the "Age of Silver" (eighth–eleventh centuries)', in J. Graham-Campbell and G. Williams (eds.), *Silver Economy in the Viking Age* (Walnut Creek, Calif., 2007), 55–98.

—— *Viking Coinage and Currency in the British Isles* (London, 2011).

—— 'The Viking Winter Camp at Torksey, 872–3', in id., *Viking Coinage*, 221–64.

—— and Dumville, D. N. (eds.), *Kings, Currency and Alliances: History and Coinage of Southern England in the Ninth Century* (Woodbridge, 1998).

—— and Jonsson, K., 'The Anglo-Saxon and Anglo-Norman element of North European coin finds', in M. A. S. Blackburn and D. M. Metcalf (eds.), *Viking-Age Coinage in the Northern Lands*, 147–255.

—— and Metcalf, D. M. (eds.), *Viking-Age Coinage in the Northern Lands*, BAR International Ser. 122 (Oxford, 1981).

Blackmore, L., 'Aspects of trade and exchange evidenced by recent work on Saxon and medieval pottery from London', *Transactions of the London and Middlesex Archaeological Society* 50 (1999), 38–54.

—— 'Pottery: trade and tradition', in D. Hill and R. Cowie (eds.), *Wics*, 22–42.

The Blackwell Encyclopaedia of Anglo-Saxon England, ed. M. Lapidge, J. Blair, S. Keynes, and D. Scragg (Oxford, 1999).

Blair, J., *Anglo-Saxon Oxfordshire* (Stroud, 1994).

—— 'Towns', *Encyclopaedia*, 451–3.

—— *The Church in Anglo-Saxon Society* (Oxford, 2005).

—— 'Small towns 600–1300', in *CUHB*, 245–70.

Bland, R. F. and Johns, C., *The Hoxne Treasure: An Illustrated Introduction* (London, 1993).

—— 'The changing patterns of hoards of precious-metal coins in the late empire', *Antiquité Tardive* 5 (1997), 29–55.

Blunt, C. E., 'The coinage of Athelstan, King of England 924–939', *BNJ* 42 (1974), 35–160.

—— Stewart, B. H. I. H. and Lyon, C. S. S., *Coinage in Tenth-Century England from Edward the Elder to Edgar's Reform* (Oxford, 1989).

Bolton, J. L., 'What is money? What is a money economy? When did a money economy emerge in medieval England?', in D. Wood (ed.), *Medieval Money Matters* (Oxford, 2004), 1–15.

Bosworth, J. and Toller, T. N., *An Anglo-Saxon Dictionary* (Oxford, 1882–98).

Bridgeman, C. G. O., 'The Burton Abbey twelfth century surveys', *Collections for a History of Staffordshire* (1916), 209–300.

Britnell, R., 'Uses of money in medieval Britain', in D. Wood (ed.), *Medieval Money Matters*, 16–30.

Brooks, N. P., 'Arms, status and warfare in late-Saxon England', in D. Hill, *Ethelred*, 81–103.

—— 'The creation and early structure of the kingdom of Kent', in S. Bassett (ed.), *The Origins*, 55–74.

—— *Church, State and Access to Resources in Early Anglo-Saxon England*, Brixworth Lectures, 2nd ser. (Brixworth, 2003).

—— and Cubitt, C. (eds.), *St Oswald of Worcester: Life and Influence* (Leicester, 1996).

Brown, D. H., 'The social significance of imported medieval pottery', in C. G. Cumberpatch and P. W. Blinkhorn (eds.), *Not So Much a Pot, More a Way of Life* (Oxford, 1997), 95–112.

Brown, M. P. and Farr, C. A. (eds.), *Mercia: An Anglo-Saxon Kingdom in Europe* (London, 2001).

Brühl, C. R. and Violante, C. (eds.), *Die 'Honorantie Civitatis Papie'* (Cologne, 1983).

Burnham, B. and H., *Dolaucothi-Pumsaint: Survey and Excavation at a Roman Gold-Mining Complex 1987-1999* (Oxford, 2004).

The Cambridge Urban History of Britain vol. I 600–1540, ed. D. M. Palliser (Cambridge, 2000).

Campbell, E., *Continental and Mediterranean Imports to Atlantic Britain and Ireland, AD 400–800*, CBA Research Report 157 (York, 2007).

Campbell, J. (ed.), *The Anglo-Saxons* (Oxford, 1982).

—— 'The first century of christianity in England', in id., *Essays in Anglo-Saxon History* (London, 1986), 49–67.

—— 'The late Anglo-Saxon state: a maximum view, *PBA* 87 (1994), 39–65, repr. in id., *The Anglo-Saxon State*, 1–30.

—— *The Anglo-Saxon State* (London, 2000).

—— 'Production and distribution in early and middle Anglo-Saxon England', in T. Pestell and K. Ulmschneider (eds.), *Markets in Early Medieval Europe*, 12–19.

—— 'The sale of land and the economics of power in early England: problems and possibilities', repr. in id., *The Anglo-Saxon State*, 227–45.

—— 'Some agents and agencies of the late Anglo-Saxon state', repr. in id., *The Anglo-Saxon State*, 201–26.

—— 'Was it infancy in England? Some questions of comparison', repr. in id., *The Anglo-Saxon State*, 179–99.

Carter, A., 'The Anglo-Saxon origins of Norwich: the problems and approaches', *ASE* 7 (1978), 175–204.

Casey, P. J. (ed.), *The End of Roman Britain*, BAR British Ser. 71 (Oxford, 1979).

—— 'Magnus Maximus in Britain: a reappraisal', in id., *The End of Roman Britain*, 66–79.

Charles-Edwards, T. (ed.), *After Rome* (Oxford, 2003).

—— 'Kinship, status and the origins of the hide', *Past and Present* 56 (1972), 3–33.

—— 'Nations and kingdoms: a view from above', in id. (ed.), *After Rome* (Oxford, 2003), 23–58.

Chick, D., *The Coinage of Offa and his Contemporaries*, ed. M. Blackburn and R. Naismith (London, 2010).

Clarke, H. B., 'The Domesday satellites', in P. Sawyer (ed.), *Domesday Book: A Reassessment* (London, 1985), 50–70.

Cook, B. J., 'The bezant in Angevin England', *NC* 159 (1999), 255–75.

—— and Williams, G. (eds.), *Coinage and History in the North Sea World c.AD 500–1250: Essays in Honour of Marion Archibald* (Leiden, 2006).

Coupland, S., 'Dorestad in the ninth century: the numismatic evidence', *Jaarboek voor Munt- en Penningkunde* 75 (1988), 5–26.

Coupland, S., 'Trading places: Quentovic and Dorestad', *Early Medieval Europe* 11 (2002), 209–32.

——'The Vikings in Frankia and Anglo-Saxon England to 911', NCME ii, 190–201.

Cowie, R., 'Mercian London', in M. P. Brown and C. A. Farr (eds.), *Mercia*, 194–209.

Cubitt, C., 'The tenth-century Benedictine reform in England', *Early Medieval Europe* 6 (1997), 77–94.

Darby, H. C., *Domesday England* (Cambridge, 1977).

Davies, W., *Wales in the Early Middle Ages* (Leicester, 1982).

Davison, B. K., 'The late Saxon town of Thetford: an interim report on the 1964–1966 excavations', *Med. Arch.* 11 (1967), 189–208.

Dialogus de Scaccario, ed. C. Johnson (London, 1950).

Dodwell, C. R., *Anglo-Saxon Art* (Ithaca, NY, 1982).

Dolley, R. H. M., *The Norman Conquest and the English Coinage* (London, 1960).

——(ed.), *Anglo-Saxon Coins: Studies presented to F. M. Stenton* (London, 1961).

——and Skaare, K., 'The coinage of Æthelwulf, king of the West Saxons', in R. H. M. Dolley (ed.), *Anglo-Saxon Coins*, 63–76.

The Domesday Monachorum of Christ Church, Canterbury, ed. D. C. Douglas, Royal Historical Society (London, 1944).

Douglas, D. C., *William the Conqueror* (London, 1964).

Duby, G., 'Le budget de l'abbaye de Cluny entre 1080 et 1155', *Annales-Economies-Société-Civilisations* 7 (1952), 155–71.

——*La société aux XIe et XIIe siècles dans la region mâconnaise* (Paris, 1953).

Dumville, D. N., 'The origins of Northumbria: some aspects of the British background', in S. Bassett (ed.), *The Origins*, 213–22.

Dyer, C., 'Towns and cottages in eleventh-century England', in H. Mayr-Harting and R. I. Moore (eds.), *Studies in Medieval History Presented to R. H. C. Davis* (London, 1985), 91–106.

——*Making a Living in the Middle Ages: The People of Britain 850–1520* (New Haven and London, 2002).

——'Small places with large consequences: the importance of small towns in England, 1000–1540', *Historical Research* 75 (2002), 1–24.

Ehlers, C., 'Die Anfänge Goslars und das Reich im elften Jahrhundert', *Deutsches Archiv* 53 (1997), 45–79.

Emerton, E., *The Letters of Boniface* (New York, 1976).

Encyclopaedia: The Blackwell Encyclopaedia of Anglo-Saxon England, ed. M. Lapidge, J. Blair, S. Keynes, and D. Scragg (Oxford, 1999).

Van Es, W. A. and Verwers, W. J. H., *Excavations at Dorestad I: The Harbour, Hoog-straat I* (Amersfoort, 1980).

Esty, W. W., 'How to estimate the original number of dies and the coverage of a sample', *NC* 166 (2006), 1–12.

Felix's Life of Saint Guthlac, B. Colgrave (ed. and trans.) (Cambridge, 1956).

Fleming, R., 'Rural elites and urban communities in late-Saxon England', *Past and Present* 141 (1993), 3–37.

——'The new wealth, the new rich and the new political style in late Anglo-Saxon England', *Anglo-Norman Studies* 23 (2000), 1–22.

Fletcher, E., 'The influence of Merovingian Gaul on Northumbria in the seventh century', *Medieval Archaeology* 24 (1980), 69–86.

Frere, S., *Britannia: A History of Roman Britain* (London, 1967).

Fulford, M., 'Pottery production and trade at the end of Roman Britain: the case against continuity', in P. J. Casey (ed.), *The End of Roman Britain*, 120–32.

——'Byzantium and Britain: a Mediterranean perspective on Post-Roman Mediterranean imports in Western Britain and Ireland', *Med. Arch.* 33 (1989), 1–6.

Galbraith, V. H., *The Making of Domesday Book* (Oxford, 1961).

Gannon, A., *The Iconography of Early Anglo-Saxon Coinage: Sixth to Eighth Centuries* (Oxford, 2003).

Gardiner, M. et al., 'Continental trade and non-urban ports in mid-Anglo-Saxon England: excavations at *Sandtun*, West Hythe, Kent', *Archaeological Journal* 158 (2001), 161–290.

Garmonsway, G. N. (ed.,), *Ælfric's Colloquy* (London, 1947).

Gem, R., 'A recession in English architecture during the early eleventh century, and its effect on the development of the Romanesque style', *Journal of the British Archaeological Association* 38 (1975), 28–49.

George, K., *Gildas's De Excidio Britonum and the Early British Church* (Woodbridge, 2009).

Gerriets, M., 'Money in early Christian Ireland according to the Irish laws', *Comparative Studies in Society and History* 27 (1985), 323–39.

Gildas: The Ruin of Britain and other works, M. Winterbottom (ed. and trans.) (Chichester, 1978).

Gillingham, J., '"The most precious jewel in the English Crown", levels of Danegeld and Heregeld in the early eleventh century', *EHR* 104 (1989), 373–84.

——'Chronicles and coins as evidence for levels of tribute and taxation in late tenth- and early eleventh-century England', *EHR* 105 (1990), 395–50.

Godden, M. R., 'Money, power and morality in late Anglo-Saxon England', *ASE* 19 (1990), 41–65.

Götz, H., *Deutsch und Latein bei Notker* (Tübingen, 1997).

Graham-Campbell, J. (ed.), *Viking Treasure from the North West: The Cuerdale Hoard in its Context* (Liverpool, 1992).

——Hall, R., Jesch, J., and Parsons, D. N. (eds.), *Vikings and the Danelaw: Select Papers from the Thirteenth Viking Congress* (Oxford, 2001).

Gregory of Tours, *Decem Libri Historiarum*, ed. B. Krusch and W. Levison, MGH SRM 1,1; trans. L. Thorpe, *Gregory of Tours: The History of the Franks* (Harmondsworth, 1974).

Grierson, P. 'La fonction de la monnaie en Angleterre aux VIIe- VIIIe siècles', *Moneta e scambi nell'alto medioevo* (Spoleto, 1961), 341–85.

——'Domesday Book, the geld *De Moneta* and *Monetagium*: a forgotten minting reform', *BNJ* 55(1985), 84–94.

——*The Coins of Medieval Europe* (London, 1991).

——and Blackburn, M., *Medieval European Coinage I The Early Middle Ages (5th –10th centuries)* (Cambridge, 1986).

Griffiths, D., 'Markets and "productive" sites: a view from Western Britain', in T. Pestell and K. Ulmschneider (eds.), *Markets in Early Medieval Europe*, 62–72.

Guest, P. S. W., 'Hoards from the end of Roman Britain', in R. F. Bland and J. Orna-Ornstein (eds.), *Coin Hoards from Roman Britain* 10 (London, 1997), 411–23.

——*The Late Roman Gold and Silver Coins from the Hoxne Treasure* (London, 2005).

Hale, W. H., *The Domesday of St. Paul's of the year M.CC.XXII*, Camden Society (London, 1858).

Hall, R., 'Archaeological aspects', in E. J. E. Pirie, *Post-Roman Coins from York Excavations 1971–81*. The Archaeology of York 18/1 (York, 1986), 15–24.

——'Anglo-Scandinavian urban development in the East Midlands', in Graham-Campbell et al. (eds.), *Vikings and the Danelaw*, 143–55.

Hansen, I. L. and Wickham, C. (eds.) *The Long Eighth Century: Production, Distribution and Demand* (Leiden, 2000).

Harris, B. E. and Thacker, A. T. (eds.), *VCH Cheshire* i. (1987).

Harvey, S. P. J., 'Domesday England', in H. E. Hallam (ed.), *The Agrarian History of England and Wales, 1042–1350* (Cambridge, 1988), 45–136.

——'Taxation and the economy', in J. C. Holt (ed.), *Domesday Studies*, 249–64.

Hatz, G., 'Tieler Denare des 11. Jahrhunderts in den schwedischen Münzfunden', in N. L. Rasmusson and B. Malmer (eds.), *Commentationes de Nummis Saeculorum IX–XI in Suecia Repertis* ii (Stockholm, 1968), 95–190.

Hawkes, S. C., 'Early Anglo-Saxon Kent', *Archaeological Journal* 126 (1969), 186–92.

Hemming, *Chartularium Ecclesiae Wigorniensis*, 2 vols., ed. T. Hearne (Oxford, 1723).

Henry, Archdeacon of Huntingdon, *Historia Anglorum: The History of the English People*, D. Greenaway (ed. and trans.) (Oxford, 1996).

Herman, *De Miracula S. Marie Laudunensis*, ii. 4–5, in Migne, Patrologia Latina 156, cols. 975–7.

Hill, D. (ed.), *Ethelred the Unready*, BAR British ser. 59 (Oxford, 1978).

—— *An Atlas of Anglo-Saxon England* (Oxford, 1981).

—— and Cowie R. (eds.), *Wics: The Early Medieval Trading Centres of Northern Europe* (Sheffield, 2001).

Hinton, D. A., 'Late Saxon treasure and Bullion', in D. Hill (ed.), *Ethelred*, 135–58.

—— *Archaeology, Economy and Society: England from the Fifth to the Fifteenth Century* (London, 1990).

—— *Gold and Gilt, Pots and Pins: Possessions and People in Medieval Britain* (Oxford, 2005).

—— 'The Large Towns 600–1300', in *CUHB*, 217–43.

Hodges, R., *Dark Age Economics: The Origins of Towns and Trade AD 600–1000* (London, 1982).

—— *Primitive and Peasant Markets* (Oxford, 1988).

Holt, J. C. (ed.), *Domesday Studies* (Woodbridge, 1987).

Holt, R., 'Society and population 600–1300', in *CUHB*, 79–104.

Hugget, J. W., 'Imported grave goods and the early Anglo-Saxon economy', *Med. Arch.* 32 (1988), 63–96.

Hutcheson, A. R. J., 'The origins of King's Lynn? Control of wealth on the Wash prior to the Norman Conquest', *Med. Arch.* 50 (2006), 71–104.

Hygeburg, *Vita Willibaldi*, ed. O. Holder-Egger, MGH SS 15:1 (Hanover, 1887); trans. C. H. Talbot, *Anglo-Saxon Missionaries*, 151–77.

Ilisch, P., 'German Viking-age coinage and the North', in M. A. S. Blackburn and D. M. Metcalf (eds.), *Viking-Age Coinage in the Northern Lands*, 129–46.

James, E., 'Ireland and western Gaul in the Merovingian period', in D. Whitelock, R. McKitterick, and D. Dumville (eds.), *Ireland in Medieval Europe: Studies in Memory of Kathleen Hughes* (Cambridge, 1982), 362–86.

—— *The Franks* (Oxford, 1988).

Johanek, P., 'Merchants, markets and towns', *NCME* iii, 64–94.

Johnson, C., 'Introduction to the Norfolk Domesday', *VCH Norfolk* ii (London, 1906), 1–38.

Jones, A. H. M., *The Later Roman Empire 284–602: A Social, Economic and Administrative Survey*, 3 vols. and maps (Oxford, 1964).

Jonsson, K., *The New Era: The Reformation of the Late Anglo-Saxon Coinage* (Stockholm, 1987).

—— (ed.), *Studies in Late Anglo-Saxon Coinage: In Memory of Bror Emil Hildebrand*, *Numismatiska Meddelanden* 35 (1990).

Keene, D., 'Medieval London and its region', *The London Journal* 14 (1989), 99–111.

—— 'Alfred and London', in T. Reuter (ed.), *Alfred*, 235–49.

—— 'London from the post-Roman period to 1300', *CUHB*, 187–216.

—— 'Towns and the growth of trade', *NCME* iv part 1, 47–85.

—— 'Trading privileges from eighth-century England', *Early Medieval Europe* 1 (1992), 3–28.

—— (ed.), *Charters of St Augustine's Abbey, Canterbury, and Minster in Thanet*. Anglo-Saxon Charters 4 (Oxford, 1995).

—— 'Lyminge minster and its early charters', in S. Keynes and A. P. Smyth (eds), *Anglo-Saxons: Studies presented to Cyril Roy Hart* (Dublin, 2006), 98–113.

—— (ed.), *Charters of Peterborough Abbey*, Anglo-Saxon Charters 14 (Oxford, 2009).

Kemp, R. L., *Anglian Settlement at 46–54 Fishergate*, Archaeology of York 7/1 (York, 1996).

Kent, J. P. C., 'Gold coinage in the late Roman Empire', in R. A. G. Carson and C. H. V. Sutherland (eds.), *Essays in Roman Coinage Presented to Harold Mattingley* (Oxford, 1956), 190–204.

—— 'From Roman Britain to Saxon England', in R. H. M. Dolley (ed.), *Anglo-Saxon Coins*, 1–22.

Kershaw, J., 'Culture and Gender in the Danelaw: Scandinavian and Anglo-Scandinavian Brooches', *Viking and Medieval Scandinavia* 5 (2009), 295–325.

Keynes, S. 'The Vikings in England *c.*790–1016', in P. Sawyer (ed.), *The Oxford Illustrated History of the Vikings* (Oxford, 1997), 48–82.

—— 'King Alfred and the Mercians', in M. A. S. Blackburn and D. N. Dumville (eds.), *Kings, Currency*, 1–45.

—— 'Heregeld', *Encyclopaedia*, 235.

—— 'Edgar, *rex admirabilis*', in D. Scragg (ed.), *Edgar*, 3–59.

—— and Lapidge, M., *Alfred the Great: Asser's Life of King Alfred and Other Contemporary Sources* (Harmondsworth, 1983).

Klappauf, L., Linke, F.-A. and Brockner, W., 'Interdisziplinäre Untersuchungen zur Montanarchäologi im westlichen Harz', *Zeitschrift für Archäologie* 24 (1990), 207–42.

——Brockner, W., Hillebrecht, M.-L., Kuprat, B., and Willerding, U., *Schätze des Harzes von der Spätantike bis ins Hohe Mittelalter* (Goslar, 1991).

Knowles, D., *The Monastic Order in England* (Cambridge, 1949).

Lapidge, M., 'Artistic and literary patronage in Anglo-Saxon England', *Committenti e Produzione Artistico-Letteraria nell'alto medioevo Occidentale*, Settimane di Studio 39 (Spoleto, 1992), 137–98.

Lawson, M- K., 'The collection of Danegeld and Heregeld in the reigns of Aethelred II and Cnut', *EHR* 99 (1984), 721–38.

——' "Those stories look true": levels of taxation in the reigns of Aethelred II and Cnut', *EHR* 104 (1989), 385–406.

——Danegeld and Heregeld once more', *EHR* 105 (1990), 951–61.

——*Cnut: The Danes in England in the Early Eleventh Century* (London, 1993).

Leahy, K. and Bland, R., *The Staffordshire Hoard* (London, 2009).

Lebecq, S., 'Long distance merchants and the forms of their ventures at the time of the Dorestad heyday', in H. Sarfatij et al., *In Discussion with the Past*, 233–8.

——'The role of monasteries in the systems of production and exchange of the Frankish world between the fifth and beginning of the ninth centuries', in I. L. Hansen and C. Wickham (eds.), *The Long Eighth Century*, 121–48.

——Béthouart, B., and Verslype, L., *Quentovic. Environnement, archéologie, histoire* (Lille, 2010).

Lennard, R., *Rural England 1086–1135* (Oxford, 1959).

Le Patourel, J., *Norman Barons* (London, 1971).

Levison, W., *England and the Continent in the Eighth Century* (Oxford, 1946).

Liber Eliensis, ed. E. O. Blake, Camden 3rd ser. (London, 1962).

Liebermann, F., *Die Gesetze det Angelsachsen* 1 (Halle, 1903).

Loseby, S. T., 'Marseille and the Pirenne thesis I', in R. Hodges and W. Bowden (eds.), *The Sixth Century: Production, Distribution and Demand* (Leiden, 1998), 203–29; II in I. L. Hansen and C. Wickham (eds.), *The Long Eighth Century*, 167–93.

Loup de Ferrières, *Correspondance*, ed. L. Levillain, 2 vols. (Paris, 1927–35).

Loveluck, C. P., 'A high-status Anglo-Saxon settlement at Flixborough, Lincolnshire', *Antiquity* 72 (1998), 146–61.

Loyn, H. R., *Anglo-Saxon England and the Norman Conquest* (London, 1962).

Lund, N., *Lið, leding og landevaern* (Roskilde, 1996).

Lyon, C. S. S., 'Variations in currency in late Anglo-Saxon England', in R. A. G. Carson (ed.), *Mints, Dies and Currency* (London, 1971), 101–20.

—— 'Some problems in interpreting Anglo-Saxon coinage', *ASE* 5(1976), 173–224.

—— 'Alternative estimates of the numbers of dies employed at Lincoln', in Metcalf, 'Continuity and change', part 2, Appendix XII, 88–90.

—— 'Die-estimation: some experiments with simulated samples of a coinage', *BNJ* 59 (1989), 1–12.

—— 'The coinage of Edward the Elder', in N. J. Higham and D. H. Hill (eds.), *Edward the Elder 899–924* (London, 2001), 67–78.

—— 'Silver weight and minted weight in England c.1000–1320, with a discussion of Domesday terminology, Edwardian farthings and the origins of English Troy', *BNJ* 76 (2006), 227–41.

—— 'Minting in Winchester: an introduction and statistical analysis', in M. Biddle (ed.), *The Winchester Mint*, 3–54.

McCormick, M., *Origins of the European Economy: Communications and Commerce AD 300–900* (Cambridge, 2001).

McGrail, S., *Maritime Celts, Frisians and Saxons*, CBA Research Report 71 (London, 1990).

—— 'Boats and boatmanship in the late prehistoric southern North Seas and Channel region', in id. (ed.), *Maritime Celts*, 32–48.

Maddicott, J. R., 'Two frontier states: Northumbria and Wessex, c.650–750', in id. and D. M. Palliser (eds.), *The Medieval State: Essays presented to James Campbell* (London, 2000), 25–45.

—— 'Prosperity and power in the age of Bede and Beowulf', *Proceedings of the British Academy* 117 (2001), 49–71.

—— 'London and Droitwich, c.650–750: trade, industry and the rise of Mercia', *ASE* 34 (2005), 7–58.

Martin, M., 'Wealth and treasure in the west, 4th–7th century', in L. Webster and M. Brown (eds.) *The Transformation of the Roman World AD 400–900* (London, 1997), 48–66.

Matthew, D., *The Norman Monasteries and their English Possessions* (Oxford, 1963).

Maxwell, I. S., 'Yorkshire: the East Riding', in H. C. Darby and I. S. Maxwell (eds.), *The Domesday Geography of Northern England* (Cambridge, 1962), 164–232.

Mayhew, N. J., 'Modelling medieval monetisation', in R. H. Britnell and B. M. S. Campbell (eds.), *A Commercialising Economy: England 1086–1300* (Manchester, 1995), 55–77.

—— 'Coinage and money in England, 1086–c.1500', in D. Wood (ed.), *Medieval Money Matters*, 72–86.

Metcalf, D. M., 'Continuity and change in English monetary history, c.973–1086', part 1, *BNJ* 50 (1980), 20–49; part 2, *BNJ* 51 (1982), 52–90.

—— 'The monetary history of England in the tenth-century viewed in the perspective of the eleventh century', in M. A. S. Blackburn (ed.), *Anglo-Saxon Monetary History*, 133–57.

—— 'The taxation of moneyers under Edward the Confessor and in 1086', in J. C. Holt (ed.), *Domesday Studies*, 279–93.

—— 'The availability and uses of gold coinage in England c.580–c.670: Kentish primacy reconsidered', in *Festskrift till Lars O. Lagerqvist, Numismatiska Meddelanden* 37 (1989), 267–74.

—— 'Can we believe the very large figures of £72,000 for the geld levied by Cnut in 1018?', in Jonsson, *Studies*, 165–76.

—— *Thrymsas and Sceattas in the Ashmolean Museum Oxford*, 3 vols. with continuous pagination (London, 1993).

—— *An Atlas Anglo-Saxon and Norman Coin Finds, c.973–1086* (London, 1998).

—— 'Variations in the composition of the currency at different places in England', in T. Pestell and K. Ulmschneider (eds.), *Markets in Medieval Europe*, 37–47.

—— 'Betwixt sceattas and Offas's pence: mint-attributions, and the chronology of a recession', *BNJ* 79 (2009), 1–33.

—— 'Merovingian and Frisian gold in England', in T. Abramson (ed.), *Studies in Early Medieval Coinage*, vol. 3 (Woodbridge, forthcoming).

—— and J. P. Northover, 'Coinage alloys from the time of Offa and Charlemagne to c.864', *NC* 149 (1989), 101–20.

MGH, *Diplomatum Regum et Imperatorum Germaniae ii.i Die Urkunden Otto des II*, ed. T. Sickel (Hannover, 1888).

Miller, M., 'Relative and absolute publication dates of Gildas's *De Excidio* in medieval scholarship', *Bulletin of the Board of Celtic Studies* 26 (1975), 169–74.

Milne, G., 'Maritime traffic between the Rhine and Roman Britain: a preliminary note', in S. McGrail (ed.), *Maritime Celts*, 82–4.

Miracula Sanctae Waldburgae Tielensia, MGH SS xv. 764–6.

Moore, J. S., 'The Anglo-Norman family: size and structure', *Anglo-Norman Studies* 14 (1991), 153–96.

Moreland, J., 'The significance of production in eighth-century England', in I. L. Hansen and C. Wickham (eds.), *The Long Eighth Century*, 69–104.

Morris, R., *Journeys from Jarrow*, Jarrow Lecture (2004).

Morton, A. D., 'Distribution', in V. Birbech et al. (eds.), *The Origins of Mid-Saxon Southampton* (Wessex Archaeology, 2005), 123–8.

Mossop, H. R., *The Lincoln Mint.c.890–1279* (Newcastle upon Tyne, 1970).

Murray, A. C., *From Roman to Merovingian Gaul* (Peterborough, Ontario, Canada, 2000).

Musset, L., 'Les conditions financières d'une réussite architecturale: les grandes églises romanes de Normandie', in P. Gallais and Y.-J. Riou (eds.), *Mélanges offerts à René Crozet* 1 (1966), 307–13.

Naismith, R., ' "Kufic" coins from early medieval England', *NC* 165 (2005), 193–222.

—— 'The coinage of Offa revisited', *BNJ* 80 (2010), 76–106.

—— 'The English monetary economy, *c.*973–1100: the contribution of single finds', forthcoming in *The Economic History Review*.

Naylor, J., *An Archaeology of Trade in Middle Saxon England*, BAR British ser. 376 (Oxford, 2004).

Nedkvitne, A., 'Handelssjöfarten mellom Norge og England I höjmiddelalderen', *Sjöfartshistorisk Årbok*, 1976, 7–254.

Nelson, J. L., 'Carolingian contacts', in M. P. Brown and C. A. Farr, *Mercia*, 126–43.

—— 'Wealth and wisdom: the politics of Alfred the Great', in J. Rosenthal (ed.), *Kings and Kinship: Acta XI* (Binghamton, 1986), pp. 31–52; repr. with same pagination, id., *Rulers and Ruling Families in Early Medieval Europe* (Aldershot, 1998).

—— 'England and the Continent in the ninth century: II the Vikings and others', *TRHS* 6th ser. 13 (2003), 1–28.

The New Cambridge Medieval History: ii, ed. R. McKitterick (1995); iii, ed. T. Reuter (1999); iv, ed. D. Luscombe and J. Riley-Smith (2004).

Newman, J., 'Exceptional finds, exceptional sites? Barham and Coddenham, Suffolk', in T. Pestell and K. Ulmschneider (eds.), *Markets in Early Medieval Europe*, 97–109.

Nightingale, P., 'The ora, the mark, and the Mancus: weight-standards and the coinage in eleventh-century England', part 1, *NC* 143 (1983), 248–57; part 2, *NC* 144 (1984), 234–48.

Notker Balbuli, *Gesta Karoli Magni Imperatoris*, ed. H. F. Haefele, MGH SRG nova series 12 (Berlin, 1962). Trans. L. Thorpe, *Einhard and Notker the Stammerer. Two Lives of Charlemagne* (Harmondsworth, 1969).

O'Connor, T., *Animal Bones from Flaxengate, Lincoln c.870–1500*, The Archaeology of Lincoln 18–1 (Lincoln, 1982).

—— *Bones from 46–54 Fishergate*, Archaeology of York 15/4 (York, 1991).

—— 'Animal husbandry', in H. Hamerow, D. A. Hinton, and S. Crawford (eds.), *The Oxford Handbook of Anglo-Saxon Archaeology* (Oxford, 2011), 361–76.

Op den Velde, W., W. J. de Boone, and A. Pol, 'A survey of sceatta finds from the Low Countries', in D. Hill and D. M. Metcalf (eds.), *Sceattas in England and on the Continent*, BAR British ser. 128 (Oxford, 1984), 117–45.

Palmer, B., 'The hinterlands of three southern English *Emporia*: some common themes', in T. Pestell and K. Ulmschneider (eds.), *Markets in Early Medieval Europe*, 48–60.

Parkhouse, J., 'The distribution and exchange of Mayen lava quernstones in Early Medieval north-western Europe', in *Trade in Medieval Europe*, ed. G. de Boe and F. Verhaege (Instituut voor het Archaeologische Patrimonium, Zellik, 1997), 75–105.

Pelteret, D. A. E., 'Slave raiding and slave trading in early England', *ASE* 9 (1980), 99–114.

—— *Slavery in Early Medieval England* (Woodbridge, 1995).

Pertz, G. H. (ed.), *Diplomata regum Francorum e stirpe Merovingica*, MGH Diplomatum Imperii 1 (Hannover, 1872).

Pestell, T. and Ulmschneider, K. (eds.), *Markets in Early Medieval Europe: Trading and 'Productive' Sites, 650–850* (Macclesfield, 2003).

Petersson, H. B. A., *Anglo-Saxon Currency: King Edgar's Reform to the Norman Conquest* (Lund, 1969).

—— 'Coins and weights: late Anglo-Saxon pennies and mints, *c*.973–1066', in K. Jonsson (ed.), *Studies*, 207–433.

Poole, A. L., *From Domesday Book to Magna Carta 1087–1216* (Oxford, 1951).

Prestwich, J. O., 'War and finance in the Anglo-Norman state'. *TRHS* 5th ser., 4 (1954), 19–43.

Reece, R. 'Roman coinage in the western Empire', *Britannia* 4 (1973), 227–51.

Reuter, T. (ed.), *Alfred the Great: Papers from the Eleventh-Centenary Conferences* (Aldershot, 2003).

Reynolds, S., 'Towns in Domesday Book', in J. C. Holt (ed.), *Domesday Studies*, 295–309.

Rigold, S. E., 'The Sutton Hoo coins in the light of the contemporary background of coinage in England', in R. Bruce-Mitford (ed.), *The Sutton Hoo Ship-Burial* 1 (London, 1975), 653–77.

Ris, R., *Das Adjectiv reich im mittelalterlichen Deutsch: Geschichte—semantische Struktur—Stilistik* (Berlin, 1871).

Robertson, A. J., *The Laws of the Kings of England from Edmund to Henry I* (Cambridge, 1925).

—— *Anglo-Saxon Charters*, 2nd edn (Cambridge, 1956).

Roffe, D. R., 'An introduction to the Lincolnshire Domesday', in A. Williams and G. H. Martin (eds.), *The Lincolnshire Domesday*, 1–31.

—— 'Domesday Book and northern society: a reassessment', *EHR* 105 (1990), 310–36.

—— *Domesday: The Inquest and the Book* (Oxford, 2000).

Rogers, N., 'The Waltham Abbey relic list', in C. Hicks (ed.), *England in the Eleventh Century* (Stamford, 1992), 157–81.

Rollason, D. W., *Sources for York History to AD 1100*, Archaeology of York 1 (York, 1998).

Roper, M., 'Wilfrid's landholdings in Northumbria', in D. P. Kirby (ed.), *Saint Wilfrid at Hexham* (Newcastle upon Tyne, 1974), 61–79.

Rotuli de Dominabus et Pueris et Puellis de XII Comitatus, ed. J. H. Round, Pipe Roll Society 35 (London, 1913).

Round, J. H., 'Danegeld and the finance of Domesday', in P. E. Dove (ed.), *Domesday Studies* 1 (London, 1888), 77–142.

—— 'Introduction to the Essex Domesday', *VCH Essex* i (London, 1903), 333–426.

St. Patrick: His Writings and Muirchu's Life, A. B. E. Hood (ed. and trans.) (Chichester, 1978).

Salway, P., *Roman Britain* (Oxford, 1981).

Sarfatij, H., 'Tiel in succession to Dorestad: archaeology in a 10th- to 11th-century commercial centre in the central river area of the Netherlands', in id., W. J. H. Verwers, and P. J. Woltering, (eds.), *In Discussion with the Past: Archaeological Studies Presented to W. A. van Es* (Amersfoort, 1999), 267–78.

Sawyer, B. and P., *Medieval Scandinavia: From Conversion to Reformation, c.800–1500* (Minneapolis, 1993).

Sawyer, P. H., 'Early medieval English settlement', in id. (ed.), *Medieval Settlement: Continuity and Change* (London, 1976), 1–7.

—— *Kings and Vikings: Scandinavia and Europe AD 700–1100* (London, 1982).

—— 'Anglo-Scandinavian trade in the Viking age and after', in M. A. S. Blackburn (ed.), *Anglo-Saxon Monetary History*, 185–99.

—— *Anglo-Saxon Charters: An Annotated List and Bibliography*, Royal Historical Society (London, 1986). Revised edn by S. E. Kelly available online at <www.trin.cam.ac.uk/chartwww/chartholme.html>.

—— 'Early fairs and markets in England and Scandinavia', in B. L. Anderson and A. J. H. Latham (eds.), *The Market in History* (London, 1986), 59–77.

—— 'Swein Forkbeard and the historians', in I. Wood and G. A. Loud (eds.), *Church and Chronicle in the Middle Ages: Essays Presented to John Taylor* (London, 1991), 27–40.

—— 'The early development of towns in north-west Europe', *Vestfoldminne* (Tønsberg, 1997), 32–7.

—— *Anglo-Saxon Lincolnshire* (Lincoln, 1998).

—— *From Roman Britain to Norman England*, 2nd edn (London, 1998).

—— and Thacker, A. T., 'The Cheshire Domesday', *VCH Cheshire* i (London, 1987), 293–370.

Scott, J., *The Early History of Glastonbury* (Woodbridge, 1981).

Scott, R., 'Medieval agriculture', *VCH Wiltshire* 4 (London, 1959), 7–42.

Scragg, D. (ed.), *The Battle of Maldon AD 991* (Oxford, 1991).

—— 'The Battle of Maldon', in D. Scragg (ed.), *The Battle of Maldon*, 1–36.

—— (ed.), *Edgar, King of the English 959–975: New Interpretations* (Woodbridge, 2008).

Smith, R. A. L., *Canterbury Cathedral Priory* (Cambridge, 1943).

Southern, R. W., *The Making of the Middle Ages* (London, 1953).

Spufford, P., *Money and its Use in medieval Europe* (Cambridge, 1988).

Stafford, P., 'The "farm of one night" and the organisation of King Edward's estates in Domesday', *Economic History Review* 33 (1980), 491–502.

Stenton, F. M., 'Introduction', *The Lincolnshire Domesday and the Lindsey Survey*, ed. C. W. Foster and T. Longley, Lincoln Record Society 19 (Lincoln, 1924), ix–xlvi.

—— *Anglo-Saxon England*, 3rd edn. (Oxford, 1971).

Stephanus, *Vita Wilfridi: Life of Bishop Wilfrid by Eddius Stephanus*, ed. and trans. B. Colgrave (Cambridge, 1927).

Stevenson, W. H., *Early Scholastic Colloquies* (Oxford, 1929).

Stewart, B. H. I. H., 'Coinage and recoinage after Edgar's reform', in K. Jonsson, *Studies*, 455–85.

—— 'A numeration of late Anglo-Saxon coin types', *BNJ* 45 (1975), 12–18.

—— 'The English and Norman mints, *c.*600–1158', in C. E. Challis (ed.), *A New History of the Royal Mint* (Cambridge, 1992), 1–82.

Story, J., *Carolingian Connections: Anglo-Saxon England and Carolingian Francia c.750–870* (Aldershot, 2003).

Strabo: *The Geography of Strabo*, ed. and trans. H. L. Jones, Loeb Classical Library, ii. (London and Cambridge, Mass., 1960).

Sturler, J. de, *Les relations politiques et les échanges commerciaux entre le Duché de Brabant et l'Angleterre au Moyen Age* (Paris, 1936).

Sutherland, C. H. V., *Coinage and Currency in Roman Britain* (Oxford, 1937).

Swanton, M., *Anglo-Saxon Prose* (London, 1975).

Tacitus, *De Vita Agricolae*, ed. J. G. C. Anderson (Oxford, 1922). Trans. H. Mattingley, *Tacitus on Britain and Germany* (West Drayton, 1948).

Tait, J., 'Introduction to the Shropshire Domesday', *VCH Shropshire* i (London, 1908), 279–308.

——*The Medieval English Borough* (Manchester, 1936).

Talbot, C. H., *The Anglo-Saxon Missionaries in Germany* (London, 1954).

Tangl, M. (ed.), *Die Briefe des Heiligen Bonifatius und Lullus*, MGH Epist. Selectae 1 (Berlin, 1916).

Tatlock, J. S. P., 'The English journey of the Laon Canons', *Speculum* 8 (1933), 454–65.

Thacker, A. T., 'Anglo-Saxon Cheshire', *VCH Cheshire* i (London, 1987), 237–92.

Thietmar: R. Holtzmann (ed.), *Thietmari Merseburgensis episcopi chronicon*, MGH SRG n. ser. 9 (Berlin, 1935); trans. D. A. Warner, *Ottonian Germany: The Chronicon of Thietmar of Merseburg* (Manchester, 2001).

Thomas, C. 'Saint Patrick and fifth-century Britain: an historical model explored', in P. J. Casey (ed.), *The End of Roman Britain*, 81–101.

——*A Provisional List of Imported Pottery in Post-Roman Western Britain and Ireland* (Redruth, 1981).

——'Gallici Nautae de Galliarum Provinciis, a sixth-century trade with Gaul reconsidered', *Med. Arch.* 34 (1990), 1–26.

Thompson, E. A., 'Procopius on Brittia and Britannia', *Classical Quarterly* 30 (1980), 498–507.

——'Ammianus Marcellinus and Britain', *Nottingham Medieval Studies* 34 (1990), 1–15.

Tylecote, R. F., *Metallurgy in Archaeology* (London, 1962).

Tyler, E. M., '"When wings incardine with gold are spread": the *Vita Ædwardi Regis* and the display of treasure at the court of Edward the Confessor', in E. M. Tyler (ed.), *Treasure in the Medieval West* (York, 2000), 83–107.

Ulmschneider, K., *Markets, Minsters and Metal Detectors: The Archaeology of Middle Saxon Lincolnshire and Hampshire Compared*, BAR British ser. 307 (Oxford, 2000).

Venckeleer, T., *Rollant li Proz: Contribution á l'histoire de quelques qualifications laudatives en Francais du Moyen Age* (Lille, 1974).

Verhulst, A., *The Rise of Cities in North-West Europe* (Cambridge, 1999).

Vigneron, B., 'La vente dans le Mâconnais du IXe aux XIIIe siècle', *Revue historique de droit français et étrangerx*, 4th ser., 37 (1959), 17–47.

Vince, A., 'Forms, functions and manufacturing techniques of late 9th- and 10th-century wheelthrown pottery in England and their origins', in D. Piton (ed.), *La céramique du Vième aux XIième siècles dans l'Europe du Nord-Ouest* (1993), 151–64.

——and Jenner, A., 'The Saxon and early medieval pottery of London', in A. Vince (ed.), *Aspects of Saxon-Norman London 2, Finds and Environmental Evidence* (London, 1991), 19–119.

Vita Ceolfridi: Bede, *Opera* i. 388–404; trans. *EHD*, 758–70.

Wade, K., 'Ipswich', *Encyclopaedia*, 255.

Walmsley, J. F. R., 'The *censarii* of Burton Abbey and the Domesday population', *North Staffordshire Journal of Field Studies* 8 (1968), 72–80.

Webster, L., and Backhouse, J. (eds.), *The Making of England: Anglo-Saxon Art and Culture AD 600–900* (London, 1991).

Welch, M., 'Cross-Channel contacts between Anglo-Saxon England and Merovingian Francia', in S. Lucy and A. Reynolds (eds.), *Burial in Early Medieval England and Wales* (London, 2002), 122–31.

Welldon Finn, R., *Domesday Studies: The Liber Exoniensis* (London, 1964).

White, S., 'The Patching hoard', *Med. Arch.* 42 (1998), 88–93.

Whitelock, D., *Anglo-Saxon Wills* (Cambridge, 1930).

——(ed.), *English Historical Documents* 1 *c.500–1042*, 2nd edn (London, 1979).

Widukind: H.-E. Lohmann and P. Hirsch (eds.), *Widukindi monachi Corbeiensis Rerum Gestarum Saxonicarum libri tres*, 5th edn, MGH SRG (Hanover, 1935).

William of Malmesbury, *De Gestis Regum Anglorum*, ed. W. Stubbs, 2 vols., Rolls Series (London, 1887–9).

Williams, A., 'Domesday Book', *Encyclopaedia*, 143–4.

Williams, D. F. and Vince, A., 'The characterization and interpretation of early to middle Saxon granitic tempered pottery', *Medieval Archaeology* 41 (1997), 214–40.

Williams, G., 'Mercian coinage and authority', in M. P. Brown and C. A. Farr (eds.), *Mercia*, 210–28.

——'Anglo-Saxon gold coinage. Part 1: the transition from Roman to Anglo-Saxon coinage', *BNJ* 80 (2010), 51–75.

——and B. Ager, *The Vale of York Hoard* (London, 2010).

Willibald, *Vita Bonifatii*, ed. W. Levison, MGH SRG 57 (Hanover, 1905); trans. Talbot, *Anglo-Saxon Missionaries*, 23–62.

Wilson, D. M. (ed), *The Archaeology of Anglo-Saxon England* (London, 1976).

Wood, I. N., *The Merovingian North Sea* (Alingsås, 1983).

——'The end of Roman Britain: continental evidence and parallels', in M. Lapidge and D. Dumville (eds.), *Gildas: New Approaches* (Woodbridge, 1984), 1–25.

——'The fall of the Western Empire and the end of Roman Britain', *Britannia*, 18 (1987), 251–62.

——'The Channel from the 4th to the 7th centuries AD', in S. McGrail (ed.), *Maritime Celts*, 93–7.

——'The Franks and Sutton Hoo', in id. and N. Lund (eds.), *People and Places in Northern Europe 500–1600: Essays in Honour of Peter Hayes Sawyer* (Woodbridge, 1991), 1–14.

——*The Merovingian Kingdoms 450–751* (London, 1994).

——'The exchange of gifts among the late Roman aristocracy', in M. Almagro-Gorbea (ed.), *El Disco e Teodosio* (Madrid, 2000), 301–14.

——'Monasteries and the geography of power in the age of Bede', *Northern History* 45 (2008), 11–25.

——'The origins of Jarrow: the monastery, the slake and Ecgfrith's minster', *Bede's World Studies* 1 (Jarrow, 2008).

——'La richesse dans le monde de Bede le Vénérable', in J.-P. Devroey, L. Feller, Le Jan (eds.), *Les élites et la richesse au Haut Moyen Âge* (Turnhout, 2010), 221–31.

Wormald, C. P., 'Oswaldslow: an immunity?', in N. Brooks and C. Cubitt (eds.), *St Oswald of Worcester: Life and Influence* (Leicester, 1996), 117–28.

——*The Making of English Law: King Alfred to the Twelfth Century* 1 *Legislation and its Limits* (Oxford, 1999).

Yorke, B. (ed.), *Bishop Æthelwold: His Career and Influence* (Woodbridge, 1988).

INDEX

Bold numbers denotes references to figures.